SPACE POLICE:
THE FINAL FISH FINGER

David Blake

www.david-blake.com

Edited and proofread by Lorraine Swoboda

Published in Great Britain, 2018

Disclaimer:
These are works of fiction. Names, characters, businesses, places, events and incidents are either the products of the author's imagination or used in a fictitious manner. Any resemblance to actual persons, living or dead, or actual events is purely coincidental.

ISBN: 9781976997938

DEDICATION

For Akiko, Akira and Kai.

THE SPACE POLICE SERIES INCLUDES:

CONTENTS

ACKNOWLEDGMENTS

I'd like to thank my family for putting up with me and my rather odd sense of humour.

I'd also like to thank my editor and proofreader, Lorraine Swoboda, for making sure that what I write makes sense, sort of, and that all the words are in the right order.

CHAPTER ONE

'WHAT DID YOU THINK about all that, sir?' asked Lieutenant Dewbush, stepping out of a briefing with UKA's Space Police Chief Inspector.

Beside him was a man who, only four days before, had been in a state of suspended animation after having been cryogenically frozen way back in 2017. But the year was now 2459, and the man known officially as Detective Inspector Capstan was exhausted, despite having had four hundred and forty-two years of uninterrupted sleep, and all he could do in response to the question was to suppress a yawn.

But his tiredness was hardly surprising. After all, since a cleaner had forgotten to plug his cryogenic freezing machine back in after doing a spot of hoovering, and he'd subsequently woken up, he'd had a number of things to deal with. Top of the list was the fact that someone had amputated his leg when he'd been asleep, and without having asked him first. In fairness, his missing leg hadn't been much use since Rebecca of Bath had run over it with her Roman Army about four hundred years earlier, but that was hardly the point. He really did feel he should have been consulted before someone had gone ahead and removed it. However, he had at least been given a brand new bionic one when he'd woken up, which had turned out to be better than his old one in every way, even if it did need re-charging every few days.

The second thing he'd had to deal with had been equally as challenging, if not more so. He'd had to get over the loss of his former life back on Earth, whilst simultaneously coming to terms with his new one in the 25th Century.

Furthermore, only about three hours after having woken up, he'd found himself reinstated as a Detective Inspector, but not in what had been known as the British Police Force. It was now called the United Kingdom of America's Space Police, since America had taken over the World back in 2341, something he'd found a little surprising when he'd been told, as he'd always thought that it would have been China who'd have done so; either them or the North Koreans.

At the same time as being re-instated he'd been put on his very first case, which turned out to be two cases; the case of Daisy the missing cow, and the case of Miss Lucy Butterbum the missing girl, who just happened to be the daughter of the man who owned the missing cow.

To begin their investigation he'd had to travel back to Earth, which he'd found to be considerably warmer than he'd known it four hundred years earlier, to visit a dairy farm in his old town of Portsmouth, now called Port's Mouth. He'd then flown to Titan, a journey of over 869 million miles which had only taken five hours, gone out to lunch in its capital city, done a bit of sightseeing, been arrested for cow murder, found himself being tortured for attempting to assassinate Titan's Leader, escaped by borrowing a large pink starship, returned to Earth, got stuck in Customs, and then narrowly escaped being blown into about a billion pieces by Titan's Intergalactic fleet of warships. And the last part of all this had only happened the previous day!

Fortunately it was Friday, and Capstan was looking forward to getting a little rest and recuperation over the weekend; but for now he was still at work, and the new case he'd just been briefed on was certainly a baffling one.

'To be honest, Dewbush, I'm not sure,' he eventually answered. 'I've dealt with numerous missing pet cases before, and, as you know, had the odd cow go walkabout, but an entire fleet of fishing trawlers?'

'I know, sir. It's hard to believe, isn't it?'

'It certainly is. As I said to the Chief Inspector, I still think that they must have been sunk by a rogue wave.'

'Me too, sir. But as the Chief Inspector said, their on-board tracking devices would've still been working had that been the case, sir. Even if one or two had malfunctioned, it's unlikely that they all would.'

'The only alternative is therefore that they were

blown up by something,' postulated Capstan.

'Or that they were beamed up into outer space, sir?'

Capstan glanced over at his lieutenant, just as they started down the corridor, and was about to ask him if he was trying to be funny. That was certainly what he would have done had the man now walking beside him been his former sergeant back on Earth in the 21st Century. That man had also been called Dewbush, and they did look remarkably similar. But Capstan remembered that the one walking beside him wasn't that man, but was instead his great-great-great-great grandson, and furthermore, that they were in space, on board the UKA Space Police Station 999, in geostationary orbit over Earth, and not on it.

In that moment he also remembered that it would be impossible for this new Dewbush to have made an attempt at being funny, as the telling of jokes had been made illegal as part of the Socially Sensible Act back in 2367. So, instead of making some sort of derogatory remark, Capstan said, 'Maybe, Dewbush, but if that was the case, their tracking devices would still be working.'

'But don't forget, sir, that tracking devices only work up to 240,000 miles from Earth.'

'So you're suggesting that a fleet of seven fishing trawlers could have been beamed up into outer space, more than 240,000 miles away from Earth?'

'Yes, sir.'

Capstan thought about that for a few moments before saying, 'Fair enough.'

'So where do you think we should start, sir?' asked Dewbush.

'I think we should start with a coffee,' said Capstan. 'And maybe follow that up with some breakfast.' He'd not had time for either that morning. When escaping from Titan the day before, they'd left behind both their guns and their police car, and Dewbush had advised that they should pop back to pick them up, as the Chief Inspector didn't like it when Space Police property went missing.

As Dewbush was equally in need of both a coffee and something to eat, he led Capstan towards the police canteen, which Capstan had yet to see, where they'd be able to sit down and discuss what their first step in the investigation would be.

CHAPTER TWO

ONCE THEY'D ARRIVED at the canteen, and had reached the front of the queue, Dewbush placed his order from what appeared to be a dinner lady-bot, and then turned to his superior. 'What are you having, sir?'

The robot in question was basically a retail-bot whose primary function was to sell stuff, and had simply been dressed up as a dinner lady. In other words, she was an incredibly attractive artificial lifeform wearing a white apron over the top of a tight blue t-shirt, the purpose of which seemed to be to help accentuate her generously-proportioned artificial breasts, which it was doing remarkably well.

'Oh, er…' began Capstan, gazing at the menu board on the wall above, which looked very much like your average fast food restaurant's menu board, back in the day. 'Do they do a Full English?'

'A full what, sir?'

'Never mind,' replied Capstan, who'd worked out by then that English food didn't seem to exist anymore. 'I'll have a well-big Americano coffee and a well-big All American Breakfast, please.'

Engaging with her new customer, the sexy dinner lady-bot asked, 'Would you like fries with that?'

'Doesn't it come with fries?' asked Capstan.

'It does come with fries, yes,' confirmed the dinner lady-bot, 'but I just wondered if you'd like *extra* fries?' and she winked and smiled at him.

'If it already comes with fries, then no, thanks,' replied Capstan.

'Are you sure you wouldn't like fries with that?' asked the dinner lady-bot.

'Sorry, but again, yes, I'd like fries, but just not the extra ones, thank you.'

'Of course, but if you order *extra* fries you qualify for our Special Offer of the Day and get a well-big strawberry milkshake for only $599!'

'As long as it comes with fries, then I'm quite happy with what I've ordered, thank you.'

'And there's nothing I can say that will help to change your mind?'

'No, thanks. Really, I'm fine.'

'Even knowing that with the extra fries you'd also get a well-big strawberry milkshake for only $599?' and she gave him another fully automated wink and a smile.

Capstan's resolve was already beginning to weaken and, with some caution, he asked, 'How much would the extra fries be?'

'As part of the Special Offer of the Day, they'll only be $399, but don't forget that you'd also get the well-big strawberry milkshake for just $599, when on any other day it would be $699!'

Capitulating, Capstan said, 'OK, I suppose I'll have the extra fries as well as the well-big strawberry milkshake.'

'A very sensible choice, if I may say so,' said the sexy dinner lady-bot. 'That will be $2,899.'

'$2,899?' repeated Capstan.

He may have been becoming accustomed to the peculiar use of the phrase "well-big" instead of what used to be extra-large, the fact that English food didn't seem to exist anymore, and that every time he bought anything, the robot serving him always proved to be so persuasive that he ended up buying more than he'd originally intended; but the extortionate prices for everything were going to take a little more time to get used to.

'That is what I said,' stated the dinner lady-bot. 'Would you like me to re-calculate your order?'

But Capstan had also learnt that it wasn't worth arguing with a retail-bot. Any attempt to do so would only end up with him being persuaded to buy even more stuff that he didn't want. So he simply paid the $2,899 by holding his watch out for the dinner lady-bot to scan.

'Thank you!' she said. 'You can pick up your meal from the end,' and with another smile, she added, 'Have a nice day!'

'I'd have had a better day if I didn't have to pay

nearly $3,000 for breakfast!' moaned Capstan, but only to himself, and being careful not to do so too loudly, just in case the dinner lady-bot overheard him. He'd no idea what would happen if a retail-bot overheard a complaint, or was on the receiving end of one, but there was something about them that made him feel uneasy, and he wouldn't have been at all surprised if, on being moaned at, this one jumped over the counter and beat him to a pulp with a spatula.

Once Capstan and Dewbush had sat down, and they'd had a sip of their well-big Americano coffees, Dewbush asked, 'So, what do you think, sir?'

Assuming Dewbush was referring back to their new case, and not the price of the meal, Capstan said, 'To be honest, Dewbush, I'd have thought it more likely that the boats were blown up than that they were beamed up.'

'I'm sure you're right, sir. But who do you think would want to blow them up?'

'I've no idea, Dewbush. A rival fleet of fishing trawlers, perhaps, one that was armed with torpedoes?'

'Could be, sir. It wouldn't have been the first time they'd have gotten into a bit of a fight.'

'Really?' asked Capstan. He'd never heard of fishing trawlers getting involved in a fight before.

'Oh, there's always something in the news about it, sir. It's because there are so few fish left and they're always arguing over who caught what and in whose territory.'

To hear that there weren't many fish left in Earth's oceans wasn't much of a surprise to Capstan. After all, there had been a significant over-fishing problem back in his day; and knowing that, he wouldn't even have been too surprised to learn that fishing trawlers had begun arming themselves with torpedoes.

But that still didn't help him to come up with an idea as to how he was going to find out what had happened to them, which was what the Chief Inspector had ordered them to do, although he'd expressed a preference that they should find them and bring them all back in one piece, as they were worth rather a lot of money, especially if they'd caught some fish before they'd gone missing.

'Maybe it would be worth having a look around where their last location was, sir?'

'What, you mean the North Sea?'

'Yes, sir.'

'Do you have any idea how big that is, Dewbush?'

'To be honest, sir, I've never been.'

'Well, I can assure you, it's pretty big!'

'Have you been, sir?'

'Well, no, but I've sailed in the English Channel before, and that was a fair size, so I suspect the North Sea is quite a lot bigger. I also suspect that if we went out there in a rowing boat, there's a good chance that we'd never come back.'

'How about a fishing boat then, sir? I've always fancied having a go at fishing.'

'Maybe, Dewbush, but we'd need a large one!'

With that, they began tucking into their well-big All American breakfast as they reflected on the problem.

After Dewbush had finished his first mouthful he looked up, and in a conversational tone, asked, 'Do you have any plans for the weekend, sir?'

'Yes, Dewbush. I intend to go to sleep and re-charge my leg.'

'Anything else, sir?'

But the question only served to remind Capstan of his wife and children, who must have passed away many hundreds of years before, and with whom he would have normally spent the weekends with.

'Unfortunately, I don't have any other plans, no.'

His answer seemed to remind Dewbush that his boss must be lonely, seeing that he'd only been living in the 25th Century for four days, which was hardly long enough for anyone to make friends, not even a rampant socialite, which Detective Inspector Capstan clearly wasn't.

'Would you like to come to London with me tomorrow, sir? It's just that I saw an ad that the British Museum is holding an exhibition celebrating the 21st Century, and I thought you might like to go.'

Capstan didn't answer him straight away for two reasons. Firstly, that although the idea of going to an exhibition celebrating his era on Earth certainly did sound interesting, and probably just the sort of thing that would further help him come to terms with his new life, he was debating whether or not he wanted to go with Dewbush. After all, he was the lieutenant's boss, and he wondered if it was a good idea for them to be doing something social together.

The second reason was because he'd just shoved an entire pancake into his mouth, and was physically unable to speak.

'We'd also be able to visit some of the sights, sir. London's probably changed quite a bit since you were there, and maybe we can see if they have any fishing boats for hire!'

By the time Dewbush finished speaking, Capstan had come to the conclusion that he'd better go. Just thinking about the prospect of spending his very first weekend in the 25th Century stuck inside a tiny cabin, on his own, was beyond depressing, and he could easily imagine that he'd end up hanging from the ceiling by his belt if he did, a position he preferred not to end up in, if he could avoid it. Swallowing his pancake, he looked up at his lieutenant and said, 'That's very kind of you, Dewbush. I'd like that. Thank you!'

CHAPTER THREE

'I'D FORGOTTEN JUST how damned hot it is on Earth these days,' moaned Capstan, as he stepped out of their unmarked Space Police car after Dewbush had landed and parked inside the Gherkin NEC. It was the only building in London that Capstan had so far recognised, and he thought it was a shame that it was now being used as a multi-storey car park.

'I like your outfit!' said Dewbush, as he locked the car.

Fortunately Capstan knew that his lieutenant wasn't being sarcastic, as sarcasm had also been banned as part of the Socially Sensible Act 2367, else he'd have been worried. He'd spent his entire Friday evening trying to decide what to buy from the clever YouGet automated shopping facility, the one built into the wall in his private quarters back on the UKA Space Police station which every cabin seemed to have. He'd no idea what people wore at the weekends in the 25th Century, and had therefore gone for what he considered to be the safest option: a pair of blue jeans and a rugby shirt with thick horizontal green and white stripes. He'd also bought a pair of white trainers, a baseball bat, a straw hat, a golf umbrella, a hat stand and a wall clock. He hadn't wanted any of those, apart from the jeans and the rugby shirt, but he'd made the mistake of asking how much the trainers were when they'd been offered to him as the Deal of the Day.

He was still worried about his choice as they took the lift down to the ground floor and stepped out onto the street. All the men were wearing clothes more like those Dewbush had chosen, which was basically his work suit but without the tie; and despite it being a Saturday, the girls all looked as if they were employed by a large corporate bank and were currently out on their lunch break. But more of a concern for Capstan was that a number of people were giving him odd looks, almost as if they'd never seen a pair of blue jeans and a rugby shirt before; and for all Capstan knew, they hadn't.

'Don't people dress casually anymore?' he asked, after about the tenth person had walked past him staring first at his rugby shirt and then down at his jeans.

'How'd you mean, sir?'

'You know, to wear something a little more comfortable at the weekends?'

'Something more comfortable, sir?'

'Like jeans, for example?'

'Jeans, sir?' asked Dewbush.

'Never mind,' sighed Capstan. He'd only bought them because he didn't want to stand out too much, but his choice had clearly had the opposite effect, and

16

he should've just done what his lieutenant had done, and worn his suit but without the tie.

Making a mental note to look up what jeans were as soon as he got the chance, Dewbush said, 'We'll take the Central Line from Bank to Tottenham Court Road, sir. The British Museum's just around the corner from there.'

'You mean to tell me that London Underground is still operational?' asked Capstan, totally amazed.

'Of course sir. Why? Did they have it back in your time as well?'

'And about a hundred years before that!' exclaimed Capstan, who'd never lived in London but he'd been there loads of times before, especially during his student days in Kingston-on-Thames, just down the road in Surrey.

Much to Capstan's relief, although similar to how it had been back in his day the London Underground had been significantly improved, the most obvious differences being that the trains now floated on a magnetic field, making them both quiet and comfortable, and it was fully air-conditioned, making it joyfully cooler than the oppressive heat of the streets above.

Barely ten minutes later, Capstan and Dewbush re-emerged into that same sweltering heat as they climbed the concrete steps up to the street, Capstan regretting not having bought a pair of summer shorts instead of the thick heavy denim jeans he was wearing and which everyone still seemed to be staring at.

As they strolled up Tottenham Court Road, heading for Great Russell Street, where the British Museum could apparently still be found, marching towards them in the opposite direction was what looked like a wall of demonstrators waving placards lit with blue and green neon lights, most of which seem to feature the skeleton of a dead fish lying on a plate, and carrying either fishing rods or fishing nets. But whether they'd chosen a fishing rod or fishing net, they were all shouting the same thing, in perfect unison: 'FISH, FISH, FISH! WE WANT TO EAT THE FISH!'

As the seemingly impenetrable barrier of people moved ever closer, Capstan called out to Dewbush, 'Any idea what's going on?'

'It seems to be some sort of demonstration, sir?'

'I can see that, thank you, Dewbush. But what are they demonstrating?'

'It would seem that they like to eat fish, sir,' replied Dewbush.

'Why on Earth would they bother marching up and down in this oppressive heat just to tell everyone that they like to eat fish?'

'It must be the Intergalactic Trade Summit that's taking place in Tottenham Court Tower Hotel, sir. Scientists have been warning Earth for years that if it doesn't ban fishing the fish will become extinct, and they're making a final decision about whether or not to ban it this weekend.'

'The fishing problem's become that bad, has it?'

'Apparently it has, sir.'

Looking ahead at the mass of people who were getting closer by the second, Capstan asked, 'Any idea what we should do about it?'

'I'm not sure that there is a huge amount we can do about it, sir, apart from maybe stop buying fish.'

'I meant about the demonstration, Dewbush! We need to get to Great Russell Street, don't we?'

'You're right, sir. We do. I suggest we double back and head down Oxford Street. There should be a walkway we can take that will lead us up towards the British Museum.'

As they reached the crossroads where Tottenham Court Road met Charing Cross Road, with Oxford Street dividing the two, they saw a wall of protestors marching towards them from every direction, looking very much like they were going to converge on this exact location. Making the situation somewhat worse was that the protestors walking down Charing Cross Road were carrying neon signs illustrating full-bodied fish, swimming. And instead of fishing rods and nets, they were carrying items more akin to what a butcher would use, like meat cleavers, hacksaws and boning knives. This lot were chanting, 'FREEDOM FOR

19

THE FISH! EAT MEAT FOR YOUR MAIN DISH!' which at least rhymed.

'I don't think this is going to end well,' said Capstan, beginning to look around for some sort of a lane or an alleyway they could squeeze through. 'Any ideas, Dewbush?'

'Um…May I suggest, sir, that we try and force our way up Tottenham Court Road? At least fishing rods and nets seem to be a little less dangerous than meat cleavers and hacksaws, sir.'

'Good idea, Dewbush,' Capstan nodded, and as they both tried to look as nonchalant as possible, or at least as if they were on the side of those who were against the ban on eating fish, with their hands stuffed into their pockets they ambled their way back up the road they'd just come down, before meeting the crowd head on and being forced to shove their way through.

It proved to be the right choice, because it didn't take them as long as they'd thought to push their way to Great Russell Street, which was virtually devoid of people, who'd probably been put off going anywhere near the place due to the planned demonstrations. A few minutes later they found themselves walking alongside the high black wrought-iron gates that lined the entrance to what Capstan was delighted to discover hadn't changed at all; the British Museum, in all its 19th Century opulent splendour.

Stepping through the gates, they both looked up to

see several giant banners that had been hung vertically down the length of four of the main marble pillars, each displaying what to Capstan's eyes looked like a fish finger, which seemed remarkably out of place, somehow.

'Do you see that, sir?' asked Dewbush, pointing upwards in some excitement.

'You mean the banners, Dewbush?'

'Yes, sir. It's the Final Fish Finger, sir!'

'It's the final what, Dewbush?' asked Capstan, without a single clue as to what his lieutenant was becoming so excited about.

'The Final Fish Finger, sir!' repeated Dewbush. 'It's actually here!'

'Really, Dewbush.'

'Yes, really sir! It's the very last one to have ever been made and has been held in a state of suspended animation since 2350, making it over 100 years old!'

'You're telling me that they're actually exhibiting a frozen fish finger?'

'Exactly, sir!'

'I don't mean to be funny, Dewbush, for obvious reasons, the main one being that it would be against the law, but I'm four times as old as that, and up until five days ago, I was also being held in a state of suspended animation, and you don't see me being featured on a banner hanging outside the British Museum.'

'Of course not, sir. But you're not a fish finger.'

'Aren't I, Dewbush?'

'No, sir. Although I must admit that you do have a lot in common with one, the Final one at least. C'mon, sir, let's go in! Hopefully there won't be much of a queue.'

CHAPTER FOUR

FORCED TO ATTEND the Intergalactic Trade Summit was the President of Earth, Dick Müller IV, as part of his duties as Leader of the Free Planet, that being the one floating around between Venus and Mars.

Obviously it was the last thing he wanted to be doing at the weekend, especially when he could have been out playing Intergalactic Golf, a game very similar to normal golf but which was played on fake grass inside giant astrodomes, so eliminating the annoyance of trees, shrubs, plants, rabbits and the holes they left, moles and the hills they built, insects, and any other living thing that had no right to be anywhere near a golf course. The fully enclosed astrodomes also meant that the players didn't have to contend with other natural elements that could be equally annoying, such as the sun, wind, rain, sleet, snow, or ill-timed bolts of lightning. Furthermore, it also meant that people didn't have to wear wide-brimmed hats along with generous amounts of sun lotion with an SPF of at least 295, thanks to over five hundred years of ozone depletion and global warming. But what made them, and the game itself, the number one attraction in the 25th Century was that they were fully air-conditioned.

Like many American Presidents before him, Dick Müller enjoyed the odd weekend of golf, although it was more like every weekend than just the odd one. Of all the possible activities he could have taken part in during his free time, attending an Intergalactic Trade Summit was probably somewhere near the very bottom of the list, beaten only by something even more tedious, like going on a sightseeing trip of the Frozen Windfarms of the Antarctic. It wouldn't have been so bad if it had been somewhere pleasant, like Florida, for example, which had some of the best intergalactic golf courses in the universe, but London didn't have any. In fact, to the best of his knowledge, there wasn't a single one in the whole of the United Kingdom of America that he could escape to. However, when he'd heard that the conference was being held in the famous Tottenham Court Tower Hotel, which was over 1,600 feet high and apparently had a roof garden, he'd brought his golf clubs with him along with five hundred balls, with the intention of knocking a few off the top when nobody was looking.

Before then he was going to have to get through a whole day of making small talk with boring politicians, pretending to listen to what a bunch of really unattractive scientists were going on about and, worse still, discussing matters relating to his planet, Earth, with alien species who seemed to think they had some sort of a say in how he managed it, just because they all belonged to the same Intergalactic Trade Union known simply as the ITU.

'How do I look?' he asked Susan, his wife-bot Series 4000, an advanced humanoid robot who was programmed to please him in every possible way.

'For a man of your age you look incredibly well, darling!' she said, with a warm smile as she helped him to straighten his tie.

That's what he liked about having a wife-bot instead of a normal human one. He'd already had thirty-two of those, and after divorcing the last one he'd made the decision that he was never going to marry one again. No matter how attractive or intelligent they'd all been, throughout the two hundred and ninety-three years he'd been alive he'd never met a single one who he considered to be perfect. And the reason for that? Because he'd consistently made the mistake of marrying humans who were, by their very nature, complicated and overly-demanding, especially female ones, and who became even more so about five minutes after he'd married them.

But his new wife-bot seemed to be perfect in just about every way, and all he had to do to look after her was to make sure she was plugged in before going to sleep and that she had a full diagnostics check-up every six months.

'What do you have planned for the day, darling?'

she asked, now helping him on with his suit jacket.

'Oh, same old, same old, really,' replied Müller, as he waited for his Chief of Staff to come and pick him up. With nothing better to do he sat down in an arm chair and pulled out his touch-tech PalmPad from his inside suit jacket pocket to take a look at the day's itinerary, which he'd been sent the week before. 'First I'm going to have to sit through what will no doubt be an insanely boring lecture given by someone called Gorgnome Obadiah, who's apparently something called a Gannar from the planet Gannymede.' He'd never heard of the person giving the talk, or his species, or the planet he'd apparently come from, so to find out a little more he clicked on the planet's name before saying, 'Although it says here that Gannymede's not even a planet! It's just some larger than average moon that goes around Jupiter.'

Swiping back to what it said about the lecture, he continued. 'Anyway, this Obadiah chap person thing has managed to start a cod farm there, although God knows how, but I suppose that's what he's going to be talking about, judging by the title of his lecture.'

'And what's that, darling?'

'How I Started a Cod Farm on Gannymede.'

'Oh dear,' said Susan. 'That does sound dull,' which it did, even by a robot's standards.

'And then that idiot Chief of Staff of mine has gone and arranged for me to have a private meeting with the…' Müller stopped mid-sentence. He was about to say "man" but realised that he wasn't one, and was trying to work out what he was, exactly. But he soon gave up, and instead just looked at his picture and said, 'the thing that looks like it's half-human, half-seagull, and half-gopher!' which was a remarkably accurate description of what a Gannar actually was, even if the genetic proportions of each species weren't entirely accurate.

Reading on, Müller said, 'Apparently he was brought up on Earth and read Biological Science at Oxford University. He went on to do a Master's Degree in Economics before becoming an Intergalactic Hedge Fund Manager for the Instathon Bank. He then moved back to Gannymede, and nobody's heard much of him since; until now that is.'

'At least he should be able to speak English, darling,' said Susan, using her up-beat, cheerful programme function.

'I suppose,' said Müller. 'I must admit there's nothing worse than having a meeting with some stupid lifeform that can't even speak the language. The whole thing takes three times longer than it should, and I'm never convinced the translators are saying what *I'm* saying.'

'You should buy yourself a translator-bot,' suggested Susan who, like all other robots, had been programmed by the company who'd built her to promote the use of robots in everyday life, and at every possible opportunity, without making it too obvious. 'I'm sure it would be far more efficient, and much cheaper too, in the long run.'

'That's not a bad idea!' said Müller, making a mental note to ask his Chief of Staff to pick one up from MDK Robotics, with whom they had a contract.

Just then there was a knock at the door.

'Would you like me to get that for you, darling?' asked Susan.

'If you could, thank you!' But then he realised who it was most likely to be, and said, 'Actually, I think I already know who it is, so it's probably better if he waits for me out in the corridor.' However, by the time he'd said all that, his wife-bot had already opened the door.

'Good morning, Mr President,' said Gavin Sherburt, the President's Chief of Staff, after he'd exchanged pleasantries with Susan.

'Hello, Gavin,' replied Müller, doing his best to sound as if he was pleased to see him, though he never was. The man was forever telling him what to do and where to go, which Müller found really annoying, even if it was his job to do so.

'May I quickly run through your itinerary for the day, Mr President?'

'No, you may not, Gavin. Besides, I have it right here, and I've only just this second been looking through it,' and to prove it, he held up his PalmPad for his Chief of Staff to see.

'Very good, Mr President, but I do have something else I need to add, I'm afraid.'

'Do you, Gavin? How exciting! But...oh dear. It looks like I'm already fully booked, right up until five o'clock. What a shame!'

'The Intergalactic Trade Union wants to have a very quick chat to you about Titan, Mr President, and with you all being here, we thought it might be an opportune time to try and squeeze something in.'

'I suppose that depends on what they want to talk about, doesn't it?'

'It's about that rather unfortunate incident last Thursday, Mr President. The one with Lord Von Splotitty, and his fleet of warships.'

'Oh, you mean the one where the Mammary Clans tried to blow up Earth, and while defending it we just happened to destroy their entire starfleet, along with that moulded pudding-shaped leader of theirs, Tim McTitty Head?'

'I believe that is the one they were referring to, yes, Mr President.'

'Well, there was nothing unfortunate about it, not for me at least, and there's certainly nothing to talk about. Titan attempted a completely unprovoked attack on our planet, which they lost, and therefore, according to Section 578 of Intergalactic Law, under

29

the heading Spoils of War, Titan now belongs to me.'

'You mean it belongs to Earth, Mr President.'

'Same thing, isn't it?'

'Er, not really, Mr President.'

'Look, Gavin, just whose side are you on, anyway?'

Gavin gulped. That was as close to a direct threat by his Commander-in-Chief that he'd ever been on the receiving end of. President Müller had a very clear code of conduct with his staff; that you were either for him or against him. As far as he was concerned there was nothing in between, and anyone he thought was hovering towards the latter category had a tendency to find themselves dying in some sort of freak yachting accident shortly afterwards.

'Your side, Mr President, of course! But it's just that the ITU would like to have a chat to you about it.'

'Fine! But you can tell them from me that Titan's now mine, and anyone who dares say anything different is going to have me to contend with. Is that clear?'

'Crystal, Mr President.' Looking down at his own touch-tech PalmPad, he said, 'Shall I maybe put something in the diary for after your meeting with Mr Obadiah?'

Müller looked back down at the itinerary still being displayed on his own.

'It says "Lunch" here, Gavin. I sincerely hope you're not intending for me to miss that?'

'Not at all, Mr President, but I thought that if we shortened up your meeting with Mr Obadiah, then maybe you could manage a quick half hour with the ITU straight afterwards?'

With a heavy sigh, Müller said, 'Go on then, but there's no way I'm missing my lunch for this, Gavin, and if they start going on and on about nothing like they normally do, then I'm simply going to walk out.'

'And after lunch, Mr President,' continued Gavin, doing his best to ignore his Commander-in-Chief complaining about having to do something other than play golf, like he always did, 'you'll need to join everyone else to discuss and then vote on whether or not fishing is banned.'

'But after that I'm done, and I can do whatever I want, yes?' asked Müller, thinking that if his Chief of Staff agreed, then he could blame him for any injuries caused to members of the public by golf balls falling on their heads after he'd knocked them off the top of the roof.

'Of course, Mr President,' said Gavin, pleased enough with the outcome of his morning run-in with his Commander-in-Chief, and that he hadn't been hurled out of the window to end up splatted out on the pavement one thousand feet below, before having his body transferred onto a boat and sailed into the middle of the English Channel to be picked up two days later by the RNLI and wind up with a coroner's verdict of having been killed in a freak yachting accident.

'And may I escort you down to the conference room for the first talk of the day, Mr President?'

'What, the one entitled, "How I Started a Cod Farm on Gannymede"?'

'That's the one, yes, Mr President.'

With another heavy and clearly audible sigh, Müller said, 'Go on then,' and stood up from the arm chair in which he'd been relaxing.

Seeing him get up, his wife-bot said, 'Have a nice day, darling,' and kissed him on the cheek.

'I'd have a better day if I didn't have to be at this stupid Intergalactic Trade Summit!' he moaned, making sure he did so loud enough for his Chief of Staff, who was now hovering beside his hotel room door, to hear.

'Anyway,' continued Susan, 'you know what they say. The sooner you leave, the sooner you get home. And you never know, you may even enjoy it!'

'That's sweet of you, thank you darling, but I won't,' and after returning her smile, Müller headed out.

CHAPTER FIVE

'PRESIDENT MÜLLER, may I introduce you to Gorgnome Obadiah?' said his Chief of Staff, as he ushered him into a very normal-looking hotel meeting room.

Sitting at the end of the table, with what appeared to be two enormous yellow webbed feet on top of the desk, and the rest of him leaning back in the chair, staring at a touch-tech PalmPad, was the thing to which Müller was being introduced. If Müller thought he was half-man, half-seagull, half-gopher from his profile picture, then he looked even more so in the flesh, assuming he had flesh, but it was difficult to tell. His skin, what could be seen of it, bore a closer resemblance to a navy blue wetsuit, and although he had two eyes, a nose and a mouth, his cheekbones, together with the bridge of his nose and his eyebrows, were constructed in such a way that it looked almost as if he was wearing a diver's mask. Furthermore, he didn't seem to have any hair, and with the skinny black business suit he'd chosen to wear, along with a black shirt and identical-coloured tie, and the bright yellow webbed feet still on the table, he looked like a US Navy Seal who'd been unable to find his flippers and so had been forced to borrow his wife's, and was now waiting patiently to be sent out on his next dangerous clandestine assignment.

Seeing the President of Earth come in, Obadiah took his giant-sized webbed feet down from the desk, stood up, and flip-flopped his way over to greet him formally.

Müller was at least pleased to see that the creature had arms with hands on the end, and not tentacles, which he disliked with some intensity, although the hands in question were considerably larger than a human's and had dark flaps of skin hanging between each finger.

'President Müller, it's a great honour to meet you,' Obadiah said in perfect English as they gave each other a vigorous handshake.

'Likewise,' said Müller, without meaning it, as he reminded himself to wash his hands as soon as he got back to his hotel room, since the creature had a very distinctive odour of dead fish about him.

'I hope my talk wasn't too dull for you?' said Obadiah, referring to the lecture he'd just given as they each pulled out a chair from the meeting room's very normal-looking rectangular table.

'What, you mean the one entitled, "How I Started a Cod Farm on Gannymede"?' asked Müller. 'Now what could possibly be dull about that?' he asked, doing his best to say it with genuine sincerity.

'Oh, you know. Some people don't seem to find the

subject very interesting, I suppose,' said Obadiah, waiting courteously for the President of Earth to sit before he did.

'How strange,' said Müller, making himself comfortable and glancing over his shoulder, just to make sure Gavin hadn't left him alone with this peculiar lifeform that not only smelled of fish but, from what he'd been able to make out from his lecture, had an unnatural interest in them as well. He'd come to that conclusion shortly after the first ten minutes of the talk, during which time Obadiah had managed to highlight the many health benefits that could be had from not only eating fish, but also doing other things with them as well, like swimming with them, having a shower with them, going out to dinner with them and of most concern, spending the night in the same room as them. The lifeform giving the lecture hadn't gone so far as to say that he'd had sex with them as well, but it didn't take much imagination to assume that he had, and with a large number, and on a fairly regular basis.

'So, what is it that you'd like to talk to me about?' asked Müller, hoping that if he could speed this up, he might get the chance to knock a hundred or so balls off the tower block's roof garden before his meeting with the ITU.

'I really wanted to have the opportunity to talk to you about fish, Mr President.'

'Fish? Really?' asked Müller. 'I'd never have guessed!'

'Cod in particular,' continued Obadiah.

'Cod in particular?' repeated Müller, as he turned around to give his Chief of Staff who was standing in the corner an "I'm The President of Earth…Get Me Out Of Here" sort of a look.

'That's right, Mr President. As you know, I've managed to establish a cod farm on Ganymede.'

'I suspect you may have mentioned something about that in your talk,' said Müller, thinking that if he was simply going to give him the lecture all over again, but a more personalised version of it, then at least he'd have a good excuse not to show up to the meeting with the ITU.

'I first had the idea when I returned to my home planet after having spent my formative years here, in the United Kingdom of America. This was where I got a first in Biological Science from Oxford University, and where I went on to do a Master's Degree in Economics.'

'A first in Biological Science at Oxford *and* a Masters in Economics! Wow! That *is* impressive,' said Müller, but unable to say it without adding a thick layer of sarcasm on top.

Fortunately, the lifeform sitting in front of him smelling of putrefying dead fish didn't seem to have any idea of what sarcasm was, like most of the inhabited Universe, and simply smiled back at him with obvious pride in his own personal achievements.

'Thank you, Mr President. It wasn't easy either, but I'll save that story for another day.'

'Oh yes, please do!' Müller said with genuine sincerity, being very keen for the story to be told any other day, preferably one several hundred years in the future, during a meeting which he couldn't attend.

'Anyway, back to Ganymede,' continued Obadiah. 'It was when I returned to my home planet that I learned of what we call The Ozeano Barne Handia, which translated is The Great Internal Ocean. I'd never heard of it before, because I'd been brought up on Earth, but then I...'

'...and then you started a cod farm on Ganymede,' interrupted Müller, who was rapidly losing his patience. As much as he didn't want to go to the meeting with the ITU, he'd quickly come to the conclusion that it had to be better than sitting through the same lecture he'd only just finished listening to about ten minutes earlier.

'Eventually, yes, that's right, I did.'

'Great! Well, if that's it, I'd better be off,' said Müller, as he got up from his chair.

'Er...I'd not actually finished, Mr President.'

'Oh, sorry. I thought you had,' and re-taking his seat, he said, 'Do continue, please,' hoping that the gesture of him nearly walking out might at least help to hurry the lifeform up a bit.

'Now where was I?'

'You were telling me, again, that you'd been brought up in the UKA, got a first at Oxford in Biological Science, a Masters in Economics, went back to Ganymede, found out about its internal oceans and then set up your own cod farm,' summarised Müller, just in case Obadiah was thinking about going over it again for the third time that day.

'That's right, and now I'm in the very fortunate position of being the owner of the largest cod farm in the universe, which is what I wanted to talk to you about.'

'Sorry,' said Müller, 'But I thought you already had?'

'I already had…what?'

'Talked about your cod farm, during your lecture, and for nearly two hours as well.'

'I did, yes, but I wanted to talk to you personally about it.'

'*Really?*'

'But more in relation to Earth's current over-fishing problem.'

'Oh, I get it now. You want to sell us your fish?'

'Well, I do, yes, but before coming to that I was going to include the parts about Earth's cod now being extinct, and how your stocks of other white fish, like bream, haddock, hake, halibut, plaice, sea bass, mullet, skate, and monkfish have reached dangerously low levels. Furthermore, I was going to mention how you humans seem to have a rather peculiar obsession with eating them cooked, often with chips, and that you used to get through billions of what I believe you called "Fish Fingers" every single day, but were forced to stop producing them when you ran out of cod, meaning that if you had some, you'd be able to start making them again. But after I'd said all that then yes, I was going to offer our cod stocks for sale to you.'

'That's certainly very kind of you to think of us, but a few things to note. Firstly, that the eating of fish with chips is only popular here in the UKA. Secondly that Fish Fingers were only ever called that here as well. Everywhere else they were known more sensibly as Fish Sticks, and were never that popular. And finally, and of most importance, that you're talking to the wrong man.'

With that, Müller turned round to look behind him at his Chief of Staff and asked, 'Gavin, who *should* Mr Obadiah be discussing this with?'

'It would probably be your Secretary of Agriculture, Bill Patch, Mr President.'

'Yes,' agreed Obadiah, 'But unfortunately I've already had a meeting with your Mr Patch, and he told me to speak to your Secretary of State, a Mr Max Timberland. But after a very long meeting with him he simply advised me that I'd need to speak to you, Mr President, which is the reason why I'm here.'

'I see,' said Müller. 'Gavin, we must surely have someone whose job it is to deal with the fishing industry?'

'I believe we did, Mr President. It was a Mrs Lucy Ward, but she left when you closed the Fisheries Department down.'

'Right. Well. Do you think we could re-instate her?' asked Müller, desperate to try and think of something to help get him out of having to talk about the price of fish with someone who smelled like one.

'I'm afraid you attended her funeral last month, Mr President.'

'Oh yes, that's right, of course. That was a sad affair.'

Müller couldn't actually remember having gone to the funeral, but he did at least remember the affair he'd had with her, which was sad, being that it had ended in tears. Not his, obviously, but hers, and in much the same way that most of the affairs he'd had over the many years had.

'So I'm left with having to negotiate with you, Mr President,' continued Obadiah.

'Right! Well, I'll do the best I can, I suppose,' and retrieving his PalmPad from out of his inside suit jacket pocket asked, 'So, how much do you want for them?'

Without hesitating, Obadiah said, 'For cod, the price is $10,000.'

Once Müller had located his PalmPad's calculator app, he asked, 'And how many would that be for?'

'For one, Mr President.'

Müller looked up at the half-man, half-seagull, half-gopher type creature, unable to hide his surprise.

'For one?' he repeated.

'That is correct, Mr President.

Müller had absolutely no idea how much a single fish would sell for at a fish market, but $10,000 did seem to be more than he'd have expected, and turning around to his Chief of Staff, asked, 'Is that a lot, Gavin?'

'It is rather a lot, yes, Mr President.'

'I see. And how much do they normally sell for?'

Pulling out his own PalmPad, Gavin said, 'Unfortunately, Mr President, I can't say how much a cod fish would, given that one hasn't been knowingly caught in several decades, but the price of a haddock, which I believe is a similar sort of a fish, is currently trading on the New York Stock Exchange for $758 per fish.

Turning back to the creature sitting opposite, Müller narrowed his eyes at him and said, 'I think your price is just a tad too high, Mr Obadiah. Would you care to suggest something a little more…sensible?'

'Considering that cod is now extinct on your planet, and every other species of white fish will probably be as well, and within the next year or so, I

41

think that is a very reasonable price.'

'I see,' said Müller. He knew when he was being played, and he didn't like it. Not one bit.

Pushing his chair away from the table he stood up, and without even offering to shake Obadiah's hand, said, 'We'll certainly give your offer our fullest consideration, but I shouldn't expect to hear back from us any time soon,' and with that, he turned and headed for the door.

But as his Chief of Staff pulled it open for him to allow his President to walk straight through, Obadiah called out after him, 'You're wrong, Mr President. I *WILL* be hearing back from you, and just as soon as you find out that there isn't a single fish left on your entire planet!'

CHAPTER SIX

'TAKE A LOOK at this one, sir.'

Capstan and Dewbush had so far spent a good few hours wandering around the British Museum, mainly in the special section entitled "A Celebration of the 21st Century", in which they'd used what had been called "The Final Fish Finger" as the key exhibit. But Capstan and Dewbush had yet to see that, as the queue had been too long when they'd arrived and they'd elected to see the rest of the exhibition first, hoping that the line would shorten after the morning crowds had dissipated.

Hearing himself being called, Capstan came away from the exhibit he'd been looking at, which featured a Dyson vacuum cleaner and the information that it had transformed the domestic carpet cleaning industry during the early part of the 21st Century.

'He looks just like you, sir!' continued Dewbush, switching his gaze between his approaching boss and a mannequin standing on a podium, apparently dressed as a Man of Leisure, an outfit which men supposedly wore at the weekends that consisted of blue trousers that were known simply as "Jeans" and a short-sleeved top with wide horizontal green and white stripes that had been called a "Rugby Shirt."

'I take it that people don't wear jeans anymore?' asked Capstan, feeling even more self-conscious about what he'd spent hours buying from his hole-in-the-wall YouGet shopping machine.

'I suppose not, sir. It says here that they were incredibly popular though, back in your day, and that *everyone* used to wear them!'

'I must admit that they did, Dewbush. Pretty much.'

'But they stopped being so popular,' continued Dewbush, as he read from the displayed information, 'when naturally produced cotton became so rare that they became too expensive, and that everyone eventually came to the conclusion that they weren't as comfortable as they thought they were after all.'

Capstan began to feel himself becoming emotional. He didn't miss jeans that much; he'd hardly ever worn them, but the whole morning spent wandering around the exhibit was making him feel increasingly homesick. For him, it didn't feel like a celebration of the 21st Century but more like the funeral for it, and the jeans and rugby shirt on display was just another nail in the coffin for an era on Earth which was no more.

But no sooner had he had a chance to read the information displayed beside the mannequin than Dewbush moved on to the next exhibit.

'Take a look at this one, sir!'

Joining his subordinate, Capstan said, 'Now that, Dewbush, was what was called a Flymo!'

44

They both stared at it for a few moments before Dewbush asked, 'Was it an experimental flying car, sir?'

'Er, no Dewbush. It was a lawnmower.'

'A lawnmower, sir?' asked Dewbush, clearly without a single clue as to what one of those was.

'Yes, Dewbush. Back in my day, gardens were very popular and often had something that was called a lawn, which was basically a horizontal plane of grass that needed cutting every now and again. And this, here, was one of many machines that we used to do it.'

'You mean people used to grow grass, as in real grass, as a hobby, sir?'

'Um, well, yes and no, Dewbush. They'd grow other plants as well, around the edges of the grass, and they'd all need looking after. It was the process of tending to both the grass and the plants that was the hobby, and which was generally known as gardening.'

'A bit like this one, sir?' asked Dewbush, moving on to the next exhibit in which a real garden had been installed, albeit one with fake grass and plastic plants.

'Yes, Dewbush. Very much like this one!'

'What's that woman doing?' asked Dewbush, moments later, pointing at a mannequin dressed in nothing more than a black bikini and a pair of sunglasses, who'd been positioned lying flat out on the ground on a pink towel as if she was asleep.

'That was called sunbathing, Dewbush.'

'Sunbathing, sir?'

'That's right, Dewbush. Believe it or not, people used to lie out in the sun, like this girl is doing.'

'You mean for fun, sir?' asked Dewbush, thinking that the idea of lying out in the sun anywhere on Earth, apart from maybe the Antarctic, would be more like self-inflicted torture.

'Well, not really for fun, Dewbush. More as a way to relax and to get a suntan.'

'A suntan, sir?'

Surprisingly, Capstan didn't seem to mind being asked all these questions, and was beginning to wonder if they had any tour guide jobs going, just in case the whole Space Police thing didn't work out.

'That's right, Dewbush. Back in my time, everyone had different coloured skin, and people with paler skin often wanted to be browner, so they'd lie in the sun in order to get a suntan.'

'But – wasn't that dangerous, sir?'

'Well, a little perhaps, but they'd wear sun cream, of course, and as I've mentioned before, Dewbush, it wasn't nearly as hot in those days as it is now.'

'This is great, sir!' exclaimed Dewbush, clearly enjoying learning all about the era on Earth during which his boss had lived.

'What about that one, sir?' he asked, moments later.

'That's what was called a Washing Line, Dewbush. People used to hang their clothes on it.'

After a moment's thought, Dewbush asked, 'Did they do that to show their neighbours what they had in their wardrobe, sir?'

'Er, no, Dewbush. They did it after they'd been washed, so that they'd dry, in the sun.'

'I see, Sir. But why did people wash their clothes?'

'To get them clean, of course.'

'By putting them in water, and then by scrubbing them with soap?'

'Not exactly, Dewbush. We had things called washing machines. There's probably one around here somewhere; but surely you must clean clothes in the 25th Century?' asked Capstan, who'd just begun to wonder if it was possible that Dewbush was having a go at what used to be known as "winding someone up".

'Of course, sir. But all our clothes are cleaned *dry*, sir. It's a process called Dry Cleaning, unlike the Wet Cleaning approach that you seemed to have used.'

'Oh yes, of course. We actually had dry cleaning as well, it's just that we only used it for certain items, like suits, and ties, and duvets.'

'What about that one, sir?' asked Dewbush, pointing at a pole stuck in the fake grass with what looked like a spring at the top and a yellow furry ball that hung down from the spring on a plastic line.

'I believe that was called Swingball, Dewbush. It was a summer garden game, a bit like tennis, only for people who didn't have an actual tennis court to play on.'

'I've seen this one before, sir,' continued Dewbush, looking down at a small rectangular shaped object beside the girl on the pink towel.

'Ah yes, the book! People used to read those all the time.'

After looking at the exhibit entitled "Summer Garden" for a few more minutes, and having read all the various information boards that simply confirmed what Capstan had said, Dewbush moved on to the next one.

'What's a "Pub", sir?'

'Ah, the great British pub!' exclaimed Capstan. 'These had been dying out even in my day.'

'What was it, sir?'

'It was a place where people used to go to in the evenings to get a drink and to socialise.'

'An alcoholic one, sir?'

'Yes, Dewbush, one of those. They used to serve them in pints, or at least they did here in the UK. But the pubs themselves were also places in which you could play games like darts and pool.'

'So they had swimming pools in them as well, sir?'

'Er, no, Dewbush,' said Capstan, looking around to see if they had an example of what a pool table was. But unfortunately they didn't, nor did they have a dart board on display, so Capstan was forced to try to explain what they were.

'Pool was a game you played with different coloured balls, on a green table, and darts were small handheld arrow type-things that you used to throw across the room to try and get them to stick into a black and red circular board on the wall.'

'When the place was full of people, sir?'

'That's right, Dewbush.'

'Who were all drunk?'

'Well, yes, I suppose it does sound a little dangerous, but I never knew anyone to be hurt by it.'

'And did *you* play them, sir?' asked Dewbush, now staring at his boss.

'Indeed I did, Dewbush, although to be honest, I wasn't very good.'

'Wow!' Dewbush exclaimed, before being distracted by the next exhibit.

'Look, sir, they've got one of those old fashioned YouGet shops you were talking about the other day.'

And so they had, giving Capstan the opportunity to once again try to explain how the process of buying something from one of them worked; by finding what you wanted using the giant-sized fully-laminated catalogues, by writing the product's catalogue number down using little brown wooden pencils and tiny pieces of paper, and after you'd paid for it, going to the counter with Collection Point A or Collection Point B written above from where you'd pick the products up.

But it was beginning to become too much for Capstan – too many memories of a world he knew he'd never see again; and towards the end of his explanation of how the whole YouGet sales process worked, his voice began to tremble with emotion.

'Are you OK, sir,' asked Dewbush, as it was fairly obvious that his boss was becoming upset.

'It just brings it all back to me Dewbush. I know it may sound odd, but I miss my life back in the 21st Century.'

'I don't think that's odd at all, sir,' said Dewbush. 'It was clearly a fascinating time to be around.'

By then they'd seen just about all the exhibits, so Dewbush said, 'Tell you what, sir, why don't we see if the queue's any shorter for the Final Fish Finger, and once we've seen that, then we can go and find somewhere to have lunch.'

CHAPTER SEVEN

UNFORTUNATELY, when they returned to where the Final Fish Finger was being exhibited, the queue was still incredibly long, and although Dewbush was happy to wait, Capstan was concerned that if he did, his leg's battery could run out and he'd have to be helped all the way back to their car to re-charge it.

So instead they decided to find somewhere to have lunch, and if there was still a queue afterwards, then they'd take it in turns to stand in line.

And so they headed off to find somewhere to have something to eat, but they didn't have to search for long, as the museum's canteen was just over the other side of the main exhibit, in the East Wing. It looked all right, and wasn't too expensive, so they each grabbed a tray and joined quite a short queue, at least in comparison to The Final Fish Finger one.

Once they'd picked up their main course, Capstan choosing a well-big Triple Cheeseburger and Dewbush going with a well-big Bacon Triple Cheeseburger, along with two well-big coffees each and the dessert menu for afterwards, they found a free table on the very edge of the main thoroughfare, allowing them to watch the world go by.

51

As they sat down, Dewbush said, 'This is nice, isn't it, sir?'

It wasn't, not particularly, seeing that it was just a canteen, but as Dewbush had said the same thing when they'd sat down for lunch in a restaurant on Titan, a few days earlier, Capstan assumed that was what Dewbush always said when he ate out somewhere, and it was just a figure of speech, meaning that it was a place that served food. So, as on Titan, Capstan decided to agree with him by saying, 'Yes, very nice!' and then mimicked Dewbush in the way he was gazing around the place, as if the canteen itself was one of the exhibits.

As they both began tucking into their meals, Dewbush asked, 'Which one was your favourite display, sir?'

'Oh, I'm not sure, Dewbush.'

'I think mine was the Pub, sir. I thought that was great!'

'Did you, Dewbush?'

'That and the old fashioned YouGet shop.'

'Yes, I suppose that was quite good,' agreed Capstan.

'But I liked the Summer Garden display as well. Didn't you, sir?'

'Very much, Dewbush.'

'And that mannequin that looked just like you, sir. That was interesting, wasn't it?'

'Very!' agreed Capstan, not thinking it had been interesting at all. He'd enjoyed everything else he'd seen that morning, apart from that. Coming across a mannequin in the middle of the British Museum who'd been dressed up just like him had been more acutely embarrassing than very interesting.

'May I ask, sir, where you bought your blue jean trousers from?'

'They're just called jeans, Dewbush. It was from that YouGet hole-in-the-wall thing in my cabin, although it did take a while to explain to the computer what I wanted, and now I know why! I must admit that I thought they'd still be popular.'

'To be honest, sir, I'm surprised the YouGet machine even had them on file! It must have had to delve way back into its archives to find them.'

As they continued to enjoy what was turning out to be an excellent meal, Capstan said, 'They're quite remarkable machines though, those YouGet hole-in-the-wall things, apart from the fact that they keep trying to sell you stuff all the time.'

'I'm sure you'll get used to that, sir. It's just a question of being very forceful with any machine whose primary programming is to sell you things.'

Another mouthful later, Capstan thought to ask something he'd been wondering about ever since he'd first seen Dewbush buy a glass of water for him the week before, when he'd first woken up.

'How do those YouGet machines work, anyway?'

'It's basically digital printing, sir,' replied Dewbush.

'Oh, right!' said Capstan. 'They'd just invented that back in my time. But how can it produce food and drink?'

'It's the same basic process, I suppose, just at another level. They call it Semi-Biological Printing, but it's not producing real food, it's more a synthetic version of it. They're still trying to replicate the actual thing.'

'And how would they do that?' asked Capstan, taking another bite from his cheeseburger.

'Well, they'd have to be able to print living organisms first,' replied Dewbush. 'They can already do basic cells, and they're able to reproduce the simplest forms of organic life, like plankton, and amoeba, but they're still struggling with more complex lifeforms.'

'Do they think that they'll ever be able to print living animals?' asked Capstan, finding the whole subject strangely fascinating.

'Apparently that's what they're working on, sir. If they could, the YouGet machines would then be able to produce real food.'

'So what they produce at the moment is just…fake food then?'

'That's right, sir, which is why it always tastes a bit like plastic. But that's why cows and other farm animals are still needed, though I suspect the time will come when they won't be, and we'll be able to print out, say, a fish, for example, which would probably solve our current over-fishing problem. They're even going as far as to suggest that one day they'll be able to print out intelligent lifeforms as well, sir, like us!'

'Humans?' asked Capstan, shocked by the idea that human beings could be printed out as easily as a hundred business cards.

'It would be the next logical step, but I'm not sure how it would be allowed, and would probably be banned the moment it was invented, in much the same way as time travel was.'

After a momentary pause, as Capstan took a sip from his coffee, he decided to ask something else that had been on his mind, ever since Chief Inspector Chapwick had mentioned it when they'd first met.

'So, time travel *is* possible then?'

'It is, sir. A couple of time machines were built quite a while back, but as soon as they'd been proven to work, the government apparently confiscated them to make sure they'd never be used again.'

'What about the scientist who invented it?'

'It was actually two people, both at the same time, saying that they got the idea from a guy called Professor Einstein, who I believe was from your time, sir.'

Capstan was about to correct Dewbush by telling

him that Einstein was a little before his day, but decided not to. He was keen to learn more about time travel. Ever since he'd read *The Time Machine* by H. G. Wells at school, he had been fascinated by the concept, and so allowed Dewbush to continue.

'But then one accused the other of stealing their idea and they had a bit of an argument, resulting in one of them using it to break the law and transport himself back in time to prove that he could, after which he vanished, never to be seen again.'

'He vanished because he used the time machine?'

'Not exactly, sir. He disappeared then as well, of course, but came back almost straightaway. It was after the press conference that he disappeared, but permanently that time.'

'And how long ago was that?'

'I can't remember the date, sir, but it was around twenty years ago.'

'And does anyone know what happened to him?'

'Not really, sir. Some people say that he was assassinated because he was too dangerous to be left alive, whilst others say that he's being secretly held inside Area 52, along with his time machine.'

'Isn't Area 52 that place where they were supposed to be hiding all that secret alien stuff?'

'You're thinking of Area 51, sir. Area 52 is just next door. It's where the government keeps things they don't want people to have.'

'I thought that's what Area 51 was?'

'I don't think so, sir. Area 51 is where they keep stuff that's not supposed to exist, like the Arc of the Covenant and the Holy Grail, whereas Area 52 is for stuff they'd rather people didn't have, like crack cocaine and comic books.'

Capstan was about to ask why the government wanted to keep comic books away from the general public when he remembered that all forms of humour had been banned, and instead asked, 'So you think the time machine exists, then?'

'Oh, I'm sure it does, sir, else they'd keep it in Area 51, but they just want to make sure nobody ever uses it.'

'Is time travel really considered to be that dangerous?' asked Capstan.

'It's probably the most dangerous thing that anyone could ever do, sir. We studied the subject at school. Were anyone to go back in time and change the smallest of things, it could have the most disastrous repercussions not only for Earth, but the entire universe! And so I really wouldn't be at all surprised if the inventor who'd dared to use it had been either assassinated or kept under lock and key inside Area 52.'

At that moment, an alarm went off and everyone in the restaurant, including Capstan and Dewbush, began to do an impression of a meerkat doing a TV ad, as they all looked around to see what was going on.

'What do you think that's for, sir?' asked Dewbush, after he'd finished his mouthful.

'It's probably just a fire drill,' said Capstan, as he took another generous bite of what was turning out to possibly be the best cheeseburger he'd ever had in his entire life.

Just then a fairly large group of tourists came running down the main thoroughfare towards them, all screaming as if the world was about to end.

'Maybe it's a real fire, sir?' suggested Dewbush.

'I hope not,' said Capstan who, like everyone else in the restaurant, seemed keen on being able to finish his meal before having to leave, especially as he'd already paid for it.

'I suppose it could be a terrorist attack?'

'Could be,' said Capstan, 'although I didn't hear a bomb go off.'

As the group of tourists ran past them, still screaming, Dewbush said, 'I think I recognise some of those people, sir.'

'Really, Dewbush? Where from?'

'From the queue, sir. The one for The Final Fish Finger.'

They both watched as the group continued running past until they reached a double door, from which burst out what looked to be the museum's security guards. But the sight of the guards must have frightened the tourists even more, as they spun around and began pelting back the other way, in exactly the same direction as they'd just come.

'It's definitely them, sir,' commented Dewbush, as they watched them run past again. 'The queue must be a lot shorter now,' he continued. 'Shall we go and have a look?'

As the security guards also ran past, almost as if they were chasing after the tourists, Capstan said, 'I'd rather wait until we've finished our meal, Dewbush, if it's all the same to you.'

But then a series of gun shots could be heard from the direction towards which both the tourists and security guards were running, closely followed by an explosion, which must have been even more frightening for the tourists, who spun round yet again to run through the security guards, back towards where Capstan and Dewbush were still trying to enjoy their meal.

However, the security guards kept running towards all the noise and disappeared around a corner. But after another round of gunfire, they all came back again, one of them looking as if he'd been shot in the leg.

'That looks painful, sir,' commented Dewbush, as all but one of the guards sprinted past.

'It certainly does!' stated Capstan, who knew all about the pain associated with being shot in the leg.

'Something's definitely going on, sir,' said Dewbush, as more gunfire could be heard and another explosion went off.

'It could still be a drill,' said Capstan, but more out of hope than expectation, and began glancing down the dessert menu as he finished off his cheeseburger.

'Do you think we should go and take a look, sir?'

Capstan looked up to see smoke billowing down the thoroughfare towards them, but as he couldn't hear anymore gun shots or explosions, and as nobody else in the restaurant seemed to have moved, he said, 'I don't think there's any rush, Dewbush. We are off duty, after all.'

'But what if it is a terrorist attack, sir? I mean, a real one?'

'Um…' said Capstan, who'd just seen that they were offering a cheesecake with a cherry sauce topping, and that it was on special offer. 'Even if there was, Dewbush, I'm not sure that there's anything we could do about it. I mean, we don't have our badges or guns or anything. It would probably be safer if we just waited here until someone gave us some instructions.'

'You mean, like a terrorist, sir?'

'Exactly, Dewbush!' said Capstan. 'Anyway, would you like some dessert?'

'Actually I wouldn't mind,' and Dewbush picked up his own dessert menu as he asked, 'What are you going to have, sir?'

'The cheesecake looks good.'

'I think I'll have the same, sir.'

'Good choice, Dewbush!' and with the decision made, Capstan got up to head over to the counter to buy one before anything else blew up. He'd not had cheesecake in over four-hundred years, and had no intention of missing out on this opportunity just because of a few gun shots, a couple of explosions, a handful of screaming tourists and a security guard who looked as if he'd been shot in the leg.

CHAPTER EIGHT

AFTER CAPSTAN and Dewbush finished their cheesecake, which was as delicious as Capstan had hoped it would be, probably more so, they decided to wander over to where all the noise had been coming from earlier. They were hoping that after all the guns and explosions and everything, the queue to see The Final Fish Finger would have shortened significantly, enabling Dewbush to actually see it, and allowing Capstan to get back to their car shortly afterwards. He could feel his leg's batteries were running low, and suspected that he only had about another hour or two before it died completely, just as it had done on Lord Von Splotitty's starship the week before.

Round the corner, the one all the various people had been running around, the place was a hive of activity, not derived from tourists taking an endless series of touch-tech pictures and videos, but from what appeared to be all four of the emergency services in full swing. There were uniformed Space Police officers in their smart black trousers and white short-sleeved shirts, various paramedics in green short-sleeved overalls attending to those who'd been wounded, the fire brigade wearing full protective gear, which must have left them feeling a little on the warm side, and last, but by no means least, the IDA, otherwise known as the Intergalactic Driver's Association, whose officers were busy handing out leaflets, just in case someone's car had broken down outside and they weren't already members.

Above the epicentre of the melee hung a giant-sized banner from the high ceiling, with the words, "The Final Fish Finger", and a bright orange arrow pointing straight down towards the floor.

'It's just over there, sir,' said Dewbush, adding with a smile, 'and there doesn't seem to be a queue at all!'

But shortly after Dewbush broke into a jog on his way towards it, he stopped dead in his tracks and held out his hand, pointing ahead, not saying a word.

There was clearly something up, and as soon as Capstan was able to catch up with him, he asked, 'What's wrong, Dewbush?'

'Look, sir. It's gone!'

'What's gone?'

'The Final Fish Finger, sir. The last one, ever! It's not there!'

Dewbush was right. The glass casket that should have housed the museum's key exhibit had been smashed, and there was nothing inside except a large number of ice cubes, all of which seemed to be melting.

'Someone must have stolen it, sir,' said Dewbush. 'That must have been what all the gun shots and explosions were about.'

'It looks like you're right, Dewbush.'

'But who could have done such a thing, sir?'

'I've no idea, but as we're on the scene, I suggest we head over and see what we can find out.'

Capstan stepped forward, hoping to be able to begin the investigation, but Dewbush remained glued to the spot, still staring at where the Fish Finger should be.

'C'mon, Dewbush,' said Capstan, by way of encouragement.

However he didn't budge, and instead began to speak as if in some sort of hypnotic trance. 'But it's out of its frozen airtight housing now, which means it would have already started to biodegrade, and after a day or two it will have to be thrown away, and nobody will be able to see it, ever again. Not me, not you, not anyone!'

Capstan was beginning to understand why there had been so much public interest in what he'd at first thought of as being nothing more than a fish finger. It had encapsulated the very essence of the exhibition, a lost moment in time that nobody would ever be able to experience again. The Fish Finger had symbolised that moment, forever frozen, in exactly the same state it had been on the day it was made. The fact that it was the last one in the entire universe made it unique, irreplaceable, and now that it had been removed from its protective housing, it was highly likely that, indeed, it *would* never be seen again.

'Don't worry, Dewbush. We'll do all that we can to find it and bring it back here, where it belongs. I'll make sure of it!' stated Capstan, with firm resolve.

'You will, sir?' asked Dewbush.

'Damn right I will! But I can't do it alone. I'm going to need your help.'

'Who, me, sir?'

'Yes, you, Dewbush!'

After a moment's pause, Dewbush straightened himself up and said, 'Yes, sir!' and went to pull out his Space Police ID from his inside suit jacket pocket, before remembering that it was the weekend, and he'd left it back in the car. 'But sir, we're not on duty!'

'Don't worry about that, Dewbush. We're still Space Police. Just because we don't have our badges, doesn't mean we can't begin our investigation,' and Capstan led the way forward to where a young Space Police officer was busy tying some Crime Scene Do Not Cross tape around a marble pillar.

Seeing his name written on the front of his short-sleeved white shirt, Capstan said, 'Officer Bagwell, I'm Detective Inspector Capstan and this is Lieutenant Dewbush. Can you tell us who's in charge?'

The UKA Space Police officer glared at the two men with a fair amount of suspicion, as he must have been trained to, before saying, 'I'm sorry, but I'm going to need to see some ID.'

'Unfortunately, we don't have any on us,' replied Capstan.

'And why's that, may I ask?'

'We're officially off duty, it being the weekend, and we've been doing a bit of sightseeing. But we're keen to help in any way we can.'

The officer didn't seem convinced, especially as the man claiming to be a detective inspector for the Space Police was dressed in a most peculiar outfit, and after looking him up and down, asked, 'And you're saying that you're Space Police, are you?'

'That's correct,' said Capstan. 'You can ask Chief Inspector Chapwick, if you like.'

But the officer had a better idea, and pulled out his touch-tech glasses that were being suspended by one arm from the top pocket of his shirt.

After putting them on, and having read the information they displayed over the tops of the men's heads, he stood to attention and asked, 'Detective Inspector Catspam and Lieutenant Dewbush, how may I be of service?'

'It's actually pronounced Cap*stan*,' corrected Capstan, 'But anyway, we just want to know what happened, really.'

'Well, as you can see, sir, the place was broken into, and after a bit of a fight with the security guards, the offenders made off with the museum's key exhibit, sir.'

'I assume they were armed?' asked Capstan, as he surveyed the scene.

'Heavily armed, yes, sir.'

'And did they steal anything else?'

'No, sir. Just the Fish Finger.'

'What about witnesses?'

'Oh, there are loads of them, sir, but unfortunately none of them have been much use.'

'And why's that?'

'The gunmen were all wearing masks, sir.'

'I see,' said Capstan. 'Any particular type?'

'Black ones, sir. Apparently they looked like the sort a diver would wear.'

Still gazing around, Capstan asked, 'And have you found any clues?'

'Clues, sir?'

'You know, anything odd – out of place.'

'Er, well, the witnesses are saying that the gunmen seemed to be wearing flippers as well, sir.'

'Flippers?'

'Yes, sir. Big yellow ones.'

'I see.'

'And that they were wearing navy blue wetsuits, along with gloves, sir, but the gloves looked as if they were too big for their hands.'

'So, they had masks on that divers would wear, navy blue wetsuits, gloves that were too big for their hands and flippers?' repeated Capstan.

'That's right, sir. Bright yellow ones.'

'So basically you're saying that they were disguised as frogmen?'

'Er, no, sir. Not really.'

'What do you mean, not really?'

'Um, well, it doesn't sound like they looked anything like frog men, sir.'

'But with the flippers, and the diver's masks, and the wetsuits, they must have looked a *little* like frogmen?'

'Um, not at all, sir. I believe frog men are short, fat and green, sir, with tiny webbed feet, eyes on top of their heads, and a tendency to say "ribbit" rather a lot, sir.'

Dewbush thought Capstan was looking just about as confused as he'd ever seen him, so he decided to come to his rescue.

'I think what Detective Inspector Capstan here is saying is that they looked like divers, *not* Frog Men.'

'Oh, I see! Sorry, sir. Yes, you're right. They must have looked very much like divers, sir.'

'Then what the hell's a frogman?' asked Capstan, turning around to stare at Dewbush.

'They're a species called Chordatians, sir, from the planet Anura. As Officer Bagwell correctly said, they're short fat green humanoid creatures who look like a cross between a man and a frog, and are subsequently known as the Frog Men.'

Shaking his head in a bid to refocus his attention back on to the matter at hand, Capstan asked, 'I don't suppose anyone saw which way they went?'

'Who, sir?'

'The frog— I mean, the divers.'

'Oh, no, sir. Not as far as I know, anyway. But I've just thought of something else though. We've been finding fragments of metal all over the floor, sir,' and glancing down he saw one, carefully picked it up and handed it to Capstan. 'They must have enclosed them inside the explosives, presumably to act as shrapnel, sir.'

Turning it over in his hands, Capstan noticed that apart from having rugged sharp edges, it had smooth polished metal on one side with a half-burnt picture on the other that looked very much like a baked bean.

'May we keep this?' he asked, handing it carefully over to Dewbush for him to take a look.

'I'm sure that's fine, sir. They seem to have ended up everywhere, even stuck inside some of the security guards, so I'm sure it won't be missed.'

'You've been most helpful, Officer Bagwell,' said Capstan, concluding their conversation, 'and I'll be certain to make a favourable mention of you in our report.'

Standing to attention again, the young officer said, 'Thank you, sir. Happy to be of service, and may I add that I sincerely hope you're able to catch the criminals, sir. It was the last Fish Finger, you know.'

'Yes, we know, officer. It's all very unfortunate,' said Capstan, with genuine sincerity.

With that, he began walking away, heading towards the exit. 'C'mon, Dewbush,' he called back. 'Let's see if there are any more clues outside. And then we can call Chapwick to let him know that we're already on the case.'

'I wouldn't do that if I were you, sir,' said Dewbush, following on after him.

'Why's that, Dewbush?'

'He doesn't work at the weekends, sir, and only likes to be called if it's important.'

'Fair enough,' said Capstan. 'We'll let him know on Monday. Hopefully by then we'll have been able to have made progress.'

CHAPTER NINE

O NCE OUTSIDE the museum, Capstan took a few minutes to have a good look around. First he stared up at the frieze depicting statues in various poses above the museum's impressive stone pillars, then down for a detailed examination of the white steps that led up to the entrance. After that he took out his touch-tech PalmPad to take a few pictures of the front of the building; but apart from the fact that the tourists had been replaced by emergency service personnel, nothing in particular seemed to be out of place. The only thing that might have done was the presence of a couple of protestors who'd possibly misunderstood the message of either of the two main protest groups they'd been caught up in on the way there, as one of their neon-lit placards stated "Free the Final Fish Finger!", whilst the other had gone with "Eat the Final Fish Finger!". Capstan was considering going over to them to firstly tell them the sad news – that the Fish Finger in question had been stolen, making the question of having it either freed or eaten largely irrelevant – but also to ask if either of them had seen anything, when he watched them begin a fight with each other, and Capstan decided that it was probably best just to leave them to get on with it.

71

Coming to the conclusion that there was nothing more to be gained from being at the crime scene, and before his leg completely died on him, Capstan called over to Dewbush that it was time to head back to the car.

After they managed to find their way to the Gherkin NEC carpark whilst avoiding the demonstrations that they could still hear going on, it didn't take them long to find where they'd left it so that they could begin their journey back to UKA's Space Police Station, giving Capstan the opportunity to start re-charging his leg.

Once they'd managed to leave Earth's atmosphere, Dewbush turned to Capstan and asked, 'Do you have any ideas, sir?'

'Ideas, Dewbush?'

'Yes, sir. About the missing Fish Finger, sir.'

'Well, first of all I think it's fair to say that it's definitely been stolen, and hasn't just gone missing.'

'Quite right, sir.'

'Secondly, I think it would also be fair to say that it was a professional job that must have been planned well in advance.'

'What makes you think that, sir?'

Capstan glanced over at his subordinate. He had to admit that he liked this new version of Dewbush infinitely more than the old one, and the man certainly knew his way around the 25th Century, but he did seem to struggle with some of the basic intellectual requirements needed to be a detective.

'Well, for a start, Dewbush, I think it's unlikely that a group of masked men, all heavily armed with guns and explosives, would have been passing the museum by chance and, after deciding to pop in to have a look around, saw the Fish Finger and decided to take it by force.'

'Right, sir. That *would* have been odd,' agreed Dewbush, and after a momentary pause, continued, 'So, sir. What do you think we should do first?'

'To be honest, Dewbush, I'm not sure. It may be a good idea to start with the costumes they were wearing. It did seem like an odd choice, to dress up as frogmen.'

'You mean divers, sir,' corrected Dewbush, keen for his boss not to get the two mixed up again.

'Yes, I meant divers, Dewbush. For a start, it must be really difficult to just walk around wearing flippers, let alone rob a museum in them. If you were going to set out to steal something as prominent as the Final Fish Finger, you'd have thought they would have chosen to wear something a little more practical on their feet, like trainers, for example. Those would at least allow them to move around quickly, especially if it all went wrong and they were forced to make a run for it. I've seen people on TV trying to walk in diver's flippers before, and it doesn't look easy, so I can't imagine how difficult it would be if you had to actually run in them!'

'Now that you mention it, sir, it does seem like a peculiar choice,' agreed Dewbush. 'If they were going to disguise themselves as anything, I'd have thought they'd have chosen something else, wouldn't you, sir?'

'Indeed I would, Dewbush!'

'Like maybe to dress up as a vampire, or a werewolf, or even in a clown's costume, sir, but perhaps without the big shoes that clowns normally wear.'

'Do you still actually have clowns?' asked Capstan, more than a little surprised to hear them being brought up in the conversation. He thought they would have died out a long time before then, especially as the whole circus thing had been going the same way as the pub, even back in his day.

'Of course, sir! Clowns are excellent performance artists, and the planet they come from is one of the most popular holiday destinations in the universe!'

'The *planet* they come from?' repeated Capstan.

'Yes, sir.'

'And which one is that?'

'Clountoune, sir, although it's not officially a planet. More of a larger than average asteroid.'

'Well, anyway,' began Capstan, thinking it best not to allow himself to be distracted by a discussion about clowns, and whether they'd always come from another planet that sounded remarkably like Clown Town, 'it may be best if we start there.'

'Where, Clountoune, sir?'

'No, Dewbush! With the costumes they were wearing. There must be somewhere that sells diver's outfits, especially ones with bright yellow flippers. If we can get hold of a list of all the ones that have been bought during the last, say, three months, and cross check them against known criminals, then we may be lucky and get a match.'

'That's a great idea, sir!'

'Thank you, Dewbush,' said Capstan, who for a change had to agree with him.

'How about that piece of metal we were given, sir?'

'The one they thought was used as shrapnel?'

'That's the one, sir. I've still got it in my pocket.'

'I'm not sure there is a lot we can do with that, Dewbush, although the fact that it has what looks like a picture of a baked bean on one side is certainly curious.'

'Perhaps we could scan it into the computer, sir? Then we'll be able to recreate what it was before it became a piece of metal inside an explosive device.'

'Is that possible?'

'I'm sure it is, sir, but we can't do it here. We'd need to get back to the station first and then make a trip down to the Forensics Department.'

'OK, I suppose we can start with the diver's costumes and then, if that doesn't turn up any leads, we can have a go with the piece of shrapnel.'

'Good idea, sir!'

There was a pause in their conversation, before Capstan thought to ask his colleague something personal that had been on his mind for a while, and which he'd been reminded of by the fact that it was Saturday, and they were going back to the station, where Dewbush had met him at half-past eight that morning.

'I've never had a chance to ask you this, Dewbush, but do you also live at the Space Police Station?'

'Of course, sir. We all do.'

'But what about your family?'

'Oh, my mum lives in the UKA, as do my brothers and sisters, but none of them are in the Space Police.'

'And if you're married with children, what happens then?'

'We can see them during the weekend, sir, and during the holidays, of course.'

'And what about you, Dewbush?'

'Me, sir?'

'Are you married?'

'Oh, nothing like that, sir. I am kind of seeing someone at the moment though, but it's nothing serious.'

Another lull in the conversation followed before

Dewbush asked, 'Do you think you will marry again, sir?'

It was a difficult question for Capstan, especially as it seemed like only about a week ago when he was, and relatively happily, just about.

'I've no idea, Dewbush. To be completely honest with you, I've really not given it much thought.'

'Well, if you do, sir, I'd recommend using Stalk, sir.'

'Stork?' repeated Capstan, thinking that he couldn't possibly mean the margarine product that his wife used to buy; at least he hoped he didn't.

'No. *Stalk*, sir. It's a touch-tech dating app that you download onto your PalmPad.'

'And what happens after you've downloaded it?' asked Capstan, out of curiosity.

'Then a little light will appear above your head, so anyone looking at you wearing their touch-tech glasses will see if you're actively looking for someone or not. It works a treat, sir!'

'I've no doubt it does, Dewbush, but as I said, I'm not quite ready for that yet.'

CHAPTER TEN

B Y THE TIME five o'clock came around on the same day, the President of Earth, Dick Müller IV, had had enough; not just of the day itself, but of the food talks as a whole, and even more so, of the ITU, or the Intergalactic Trade Union as they liked to be called.

Not only had he had to attend a two hour-long lecture about how some half-man, half-seagull, half-gopher type lifeform had started a cod farm on Ganymede that had been given the highly imaginative title of, "How I Started A Cod Farm On Ganymede", he'd then had to sit through a meeting with the fish-smelling lifeform that had given the lecture, who at the end had had the contemptible audacity to propose to sell him cod at a cost of $10,000 per fish, which Müller felt was about ten times more than it should have been.

Following that, he'd been forced to sit around a very boring-looking table, with nineteen equally boring-looking aliens, whilst they lectured him about the morals and legalities of destroying the entire fleet of Mammary Clans, including their Commander-in-Chief, Lord Von Splotitty, after which he'd declared to them and the rest of the universe that Titan now belonged to him. He'd concluded that particular meeting by telling them all how much he appreciated their remarks and concerns but that basically they could all get stuffed.

Once he'd walked out of that meeting, Müller was forced to have his lunch in a canteen, of all places! And after that truly horrific ordeal, he'd snuck up to the roof garden with his golf clubs and a hundred balls with the intention of knocking a few off the top, but not only was there a large flashing neon sign that stated, "NO BALL GAMES, AND THAT INCLUDES GOLF!" but there were also four formidable-looking security-bots standing in each corner of the garden, clearly keen to make sure that the neon letter of the roof garden's law was upheld. Subsequently he'd been forced to say that he was lost and had asked them if they knew where the toilets were.

But the icing on the cake had been when he'd had to sit through no less than a four hour debate about whether or not Planet Earth should ban fishing, after which a vote was taken. To Müller's disgust, everyone decided to vote against his wishes, which had been to keep fishing until every last fish was dead, by which time, he'd argued, technology would have come to the rescue in the form of Biological Digital Printing, allowing people to print out just as many fish as they wanted, whenever they wanted them.

So, with fishing banned against his will, with him not looking as if he was going to have the chance to hit a single golf ball for the entire weekend, and with the second day of the summit looking even more dull than the current one, as a lengthy talk had already been planned to discuss how they were going to pacify all the fishermen who'd just found themselves out of work, what everyone was going to eat instead of fish, and how they were going to shore up the potato chip industry, which would no doubt be in freefall with no more fish to go with the billions of tonnes of chips they produced each day, he'd just announced to Gavin that he was leaving.

'But, er, Mr President, you can't just, er…'

Gavin was about to say that he couldn't just leave, but seeing the look on his Commander-in-Chief's face, he made the executive decision that he wasn't paid enough to tell him.

'I can't *what?*' asked Müller, almost daring him to say it.

'Er, what I meant to say, Mr President, was that you can do anything you like. You are, after all, the President of Earth.'

'Damn right I am!' stated Müller, returning his attention back to sorting out his golf bag while his wife-bot was packing up everything else over on the other side of their ornately-decorated room. 'And besides,' he continued, 'I really have no choice. If I was forced to stay in this garish monstrosity of a so-called hotel for one more day, jammed in with the ITU and just about everyone else, I suspect I'd end up throwing myself off the roof, and as there's no sign up there saying I can't, unlike other things I could mention, I'd probably be allowed to!'

Gavin found the idea of Dick Müller IV throwing himself off a building that was well over a thousand feet tall rather hard to believe, and even if he did, he'd only do so having made sure that there was at least one robotic device on the ground ready to catch him.

'Of course, Mr President,' said Gavin, 'but wouldn't you at least like to stay the night? There is, after all, going to be a lavish dinner in your honour, followed by a dance that I'm sure your wife-bot would enjoy.'

'She has a name, you know!' stated Müller.

He really didn't like it when his wife, who wasn't actually his wife, although she would have been if he'd married her, was called a wife-bot. Even though she was, he felt it both insulting and highly disrespectful to both his and her good name.

'Sorry, Mr President. Of course I meant to say, er, Susan.'

On hearing her name, the President's wife-bot turned around, and with an enchanting smile, said, 'Oh, hello, Gavin! I didn't see you there,' before returning to what she'd been doing before, which was removing all of her registered owner's socks from the sock draw to pack them carefully away in one of the three bespoke Gucci suitcases that had been handcrafted especially for them.

'Anyway, we're leaving, and that's final!' stated Müller, just as he found the last golf ball he'd been looking for which was under the sofa. And as he popped it into the correct zipped pocket, he heaved his giant-sized golf bag onto his shoulder and began marching towards the hotel suite's door, where Gavin was standing, as he was paid to. And as he gave Gavin a very hard stare, he called out behind him, 'It's time to go, Susan, darling.'

'OK, darling,' replied Susan. 'Just give me 3.2 seconds and I'll be with you,' and she switched her current function setting up from basic "Packing" to "Well-Quick Packing". And with her limbs now moving at such a pace that they became a blur, exactly 3.2 seconds later she'd closed the last of three suitcases, had placed one on top of the other and was wheeling them towards the hotel room door without even breaking into a sweat, or at least without having overheated any of her complex circuitry.

Seeing the President, and the wife-bot who was already beginning to be known as the First Lady, marching towards him, Gavin thought it better if he just opened the door for them and stood to one side to allow them through.

'If you could have our car waiting for us outside,'

said Müller, as he breezed straight past him, heading for the lift, 'I'd appreciate that.'

However, the President's request wasn't as simple as it might have sounded. The President's car was just one of a whole fleet of vehicles that always travelled around together, apart from when it had to go in for its MOT of course, but when it did that, it didn't have the President sitting inside it.

'I'll get straight on to it,' replied Gavin, as he watched President Müller and his wife-bot step into the first available lift. The moment the doors closed, he moved to the next one over and pushed the button, and began to make a series of frantic phone calls, raising the alarm to the President's Secret Service team, the hotel's staff, and the UKA's Space Police, that their President was on the move.

By the time Gavin made it down to the lobby, the President and his wife-bot had almost reached the Tottenham Court Tower Hotel's doors, and he leapt forward in a bid to stop them from going outside until the Secret Service team arrived. As he did so, he desperately tried to think of something to say that would stop the President from walking out without actually having to tell him not to.

But fortunately for Gavin, the moment Müller placed his hand on the highly polished brass door handle, a meat cleaver embedded itself in the varnished oak door frame outside which would have buried itself into Müller's upper left thorax, had it not been for the door getting in its way.

'What the…' began Müller, somewhat surprised, and took the precaution of peering outside before going any further.

On the street below the steps leading up to the hotel's entrance were the demonstrations that Capstan and Dewbush had been caught up in earlier that day. News had already leaked out that fishing had been banned throughout the entire planet, and the protestors who'd been against the ban had since launched an all-out attack on the protestors who'd been in favour. Despite the fact that those who'd been in favour, who'd been chanting, "FREEDOM FOR THE FISH! EAT MEAT FOR YOUR MAIN DISH!" were more heavily armed, the "against" protest party had overcome them through sheer weight of numbers, taking heavy casualties as they'd done so. And having won that particular battle the fish eaters now assembled themselves outside the hotel where the vote had been taken, chanting, "FISH, FISH, FISH! WE WANT TO EAT THE FISH!" so loudly that the hotel's ground floor windows began to vibrate. And to back up their message they started hurling a variety of kitchen utensils at the doors whenever they saw someone's head peering through. One of those objects had included the meat cleaver that looked as if it was going to be left embedded in the doorframe to serve as a warning to any politician who dared take a step outside.

Taking a quick peek through the glass doors himself, it was clear from Gavin's perspective that the mob were worth taking seriously, and judging by the blood and injuries some of them seemed to have already sustained, could easily be prepared to fight for their cause, possibly to the death, to leave them in much the same way as they'd have liked to have seen Earth's remaining supply of fish: battered, fried in oil, wrapped up in paper and served with chips and some tomato ketchup.

'It may be better if you leave via the back door,' suggested Gavin, and then thought to risk adding, 'or maybe you should stay the night and think about leaving in the morning?'

But just the hint that decisions were being made for him, either by his Chief of Staff, or the mob outside the hotel, only served to make Müller even more belligerent than normal.

'No, Gavin! I'm not scared of a bunch of fish-eating activists. I'm going out the front!'

Setting his golf bag down on the ornately-decorated marble floor he pulled out his 7 iron, a club that had seen him through many a sticky situation; at least it had done on the golf course. And after taking a firm hold of it using the correct overlapping grip, he began swinging it about, preparing himself to take out some of his pent up aggression on the crowd outside.

Seeing what he was doing, Susan asked, 'May I join you?' as she examined the remaining clubs to see which one would make the most suitable weapon for her to use.

Müller stared at her with new admiration. A woman who not only had a right hand that could vibrate at five different speed settings, but also one who was prepared to stand by him, side by side, against what looked like an unassailable force, armed only with what she was pulling out of his golf bag, which he noted was a Watson ProElite Sand Wedge with a diamond cut face, a carbon fibre handle and a full-leather grip, was a woman to be proud of, even if she wasn't a real one. He took a moment to watch her as she began slicing it through the air, like a sword being wielded by a 25th Century robotic version of Boadicea, the Celtic British Queen who'd led a suicide mission against the entire Roman Empire back in AD 61.

'By all means!' Müller replied, thinking that she was looking so dangerous that he might even be inclined to let her go out first.

Horrified by what he was seeing, that both the President of Earth and his First Lady seemed to be preparing themselves to enter into a combat situation armed only with a couple of golf clubs against what must be several thousand disgruntled protestors, most of whom were wielding meat cleavers, hacksaws or boning knives, Gavin was about to try and talk at least his President out of it, but realised that it would be pointless, and would probably only serve to exacerbate the situation. He wasn't sure how the situation could be exacerbated, but he wasn't going to risk it, and instead said, 'Mr President, if you could just wait for your Secret Service team, I'm sure you'd stand a much better chance.'

But Müller was seeing red, and pleased to have finally found a good excuse to swing a golf club around, said, 'I think I'd rather go now.' He then placed his hand back on the door handle and glancing back over at his wife-bot, said, 'Death and glory. What do you say, darling?'

Susan, who was now swinging the club back and forth with such venom and with such incredible velocity that she was beginning to look more dangerous than his entire Secret Service put together, simply said, 'Sounds good to me, darling,' and gave him a cheeky wink and a smile.

With his heart bursting with pride for this relatively new woman in his life, Müller turned his attention back to the baying crowd on the street below and decided, there and then, that if they both survived he'd propose to her.

Without further ado, he pushed open the door, and with a sound like that of a five year old Tyrannosaurus Rex having a tantrum, charged down the steps towards the crowd, all seven thousand, four hundred and forty nine of them, with Susan leaping down after him.

From the protestors' perspective, of all the people they were expecting to be charged by, the President of Earth, Dick Müller IV, and the robot most of them now considered to be their First Lady were definitely not two of them, and they were momentarily taken off guard, allowing Müller and his wife-bot to do some significant damage, and to a fair few of them as well.

However, as soon as they realised that there were only two of them, and they only had a couple of golf clubs as weapons, they surged forward, and began to put up quite a good fight.

To Gavin's huge relief, at that moment the wail of UKA Space Police sirens could be heard, but even more comforting was the clatter of the President's Secret Service, all ex-Special Forces and all armed with MDK 12mm Decapitators, closely followed by about half a dozen of the hotel's security-bots, who weren't Special Forces but were running on a programme designed by one of them, and each had the MDK 16mm Exterminator, the larger version of the one the President's Secret Service team had. Within a moment or two of entering the lobby, both groups had assessed the situation out on the street and subsequently piled through the hotel doors to begin putting their years of training and advanced military programming to good use whilst shouting, 'PROTECT THE PRESIDENT,

AND THE FIRST LADY!' as they did so, even though it didn't look as if they needed much protecting at all.

With this vicious and quite merciless onslaught from Earth's President, his wife-bot Series 4000, the ex-Special Forces Secret Service, and six hotel Special Forces-programmed security-bots, plus the noise of the sirens closing in from above, the crowd of demonstrators did the only thing that any right-minded human being would do under such overwhelming circumstances, and threw down any weapon they had to attempt to make a run for it.

CHAPTER ELEVEN

O N ARRIVING BACK at the UKA's Space Police Station 999, Capstan and Dewbush were a little disappointed to discover that the Forensics Department was closed for the weekend, and although the door wasn't locked, not even Dewbush knew how to scan the fragment of metal they'd been given into the computer, and then ask it to use that to recreate what it had been before. So, instead they popped it into a plastic bag and left it in the middle of one of the Forensics team's desk with a note underneath, which Dewbush wrote, saying, "Can you please scan this piece of metal into the computer and then ask it to recreate what it used to be before it was a piece of metal, thanks!' And underneath that he'd written out his own name, and that of Detective Inspector Capstan, so that they'd know who to contact when they had a chance to do it and the results came through.

Then they sat at one of the department's larger computers, which had a wall-sized monitor, and ran a database search for places in the universe that sold human diver's outfits. Once found, they narrowed that down to a list of all the people who'd bought one during the last three months, and then ran that against the Space Police's main criminal database.

After three hours of hard work, they were delighted to come up with a name; that of Mr Daniel Dumbarton who lived in the Cornish coastal town of Padstow. According to the sales receipt, he'd bought five sets of scuba diving equipment just two weeks before, including masks, navy blue wetsuits and large yellow flippers. He also had a criminal record, and although it was only for not returning a library data file, it was at least a criminal offence which, as far as Capstan was concerned, was good enough to make him the prime suspect in the Case of the Stolen Fish Finger.

But now they had to wait for Monday to get clearance from Chief Inspector Chapwick to continue their investigation, so they spent the evening at a Space Police bar called 'Ave 'Em, during which time Dewbush was able to persuade Capstan to download the Stalk app he'd mentioned earlier that day, but only after Capstan had had three glasses of Milf, a trendy new drink that was a combination of coconut milk, vanilla ice cream and rum. And when they'd both had a few more, Dewbush taught him how to use the app, so that he could "stalk" other users, and gave him a demonstration which ended up with him being slapped across the face when he followed an attractive young female Space Police officer into the women's toilets.

The following day being a Sunday, after they both

had a bit of a lie in, Dewbush took Capstan on the full tour of the Space Police Station, and spent the afternoon in the shooting range with him, giving him his very first lesson in how to use a firearm, in particular the MDK 12mm Decapitator that was the standard issue gun for the Space Police as well as for a vast number of other military organisations on Earth, and further afield.

Once Capstan had the feel of how to load and shoot it, with varying degrees of success, Dewbush moved him on to having a go with the gun's big brother, the 16mm Annihilator, which proved a little too much for him, as firing it had a tendency to leave him lying flat on his back, knocked to the floor by the recoil. Fortunately, the firing range had the same spongy white flooring as the rest of the Space Police Station, so no harm was done; but Capstan was left feeling rather stupid, and after having a few goes, all of which left him in the same position, he decided that he'd better just stick with the 12mm version.

For the evening, Capstan thought he'd spend a quiet few hours inside his cabin, sorting through some of the many items he'd been persuaded into buying from his YouGet hole-in-the-wall shopping facility, and was going to bite the bullet and do a Dongle search for his wife and children using his PalmPad when he was amazed to come across an advert for something called eBay Intergalactic, that seemed to be the same in just about every respect as the eBay he'd known, apart from the items it was selling and the fact that it appeared to cater for a much wider audience.

After registering, he took a picture of the hat stand which he'd bought during his first go at using his YouGet hole in the wall, and which was the largest item he had and was subsequently taking up the most space. And once that item had been posted up, he turned in for an early night, to make sure that both he and his leg were charged up, ready for the start of what would only be his second week as a Detective Inspector for the Space Police.

CHAPTER TWELVE

AT HALF PAST eight the next morning, Dewbush swung by Capstan's cabin as he was beginning to make a habit of doing. They'd arranged a meeting with Chief Inspector Chapwick, via his PA, for half past nine, and Capstan was keen to have some breakfast and a coffee first, not only for a chance to wake up, but also to go over what they wanted to ask Chapwick permission for; to head down to Padstow to interview, and possibly bring in for questioning, the man they'd identified on Saturday as having purchased five sets of scuba diving outfits two weeks previously, Mr Daniel Dumbarton.

'How are you getting on with those missing fishing trawlers?' asked Chapwick, once Capstan and Dewbush managed to find the two virtually invisible chairs in front of his almost invisible desk, and sat down safely in them.

'OK,' replied Capstan, which was about as vague a response as he could think of, seeing that they hadn't made any progress at all, as they hadn't started. 'But we've actually just begun working on another case that we believe is linked, sir.'

There was no evidence to suggest that the case of the missing fishing trawlers had anything to do with the case of the Stolen Fish Finger, other than the obvious: that they both involved either fish or fishing. But Capstan knew what Chapwick would say if he told the truth, that they'd spent their entire weekend working on a case that he hadn't assigned them, whilst ignoring the one he had, and it wouldn't be good.

'That sounds encouraging,' said Chapwick. 'And which case is that?'

'The case of the Stolen Fish Finger, sir!' announced Capstan. 'The one that was taken by a gang of armed robbers from the British Museum on Saturday.'

'Ah yes! Well, of course I've been informed about that. But why do you think they're connected?'

'Because of the link to fish, sir, and also because Dewbush and I just happened to be there when the Final Fish Finger was stolen, sir.'

'You were at the British Museum on Saturday morning, were you?' asked Chapwick.

'Yes, sir. Lieutenant Dewbush had kindly informed me of an exhibition they are holding about the 21st Century, so we'd popped down to take a look on our day off, sir.'

'That was a piece of good fortune!'

'It was, sir, yes! And because we were there, we've already made excellent progress in finding out who the criminals behind it are, sir.'

'What, already!' exclaimed Chapwick, who couldn't help but give Capstan and Dewbush a broad smile. It had been an unusual decision for him to allow the man from the 21st Century to be fully defrosted, and then to assign him straight into the Space Police as a Detective Inspector. He'd even taken some flack over it from the Department of Justice, who'd only agreed because the subject in question had been awarded an OBE and two Queen's Police Medals during his time with the British Police. So Chapwick was even more pleased than he would have normally been that they'd made progress, especially as they'd done so on their day off.

'And what have you found out so far?' he asked, eager to learn more.

'Well, sir, there are two lines of enquiries we're currently following. The first is the unusual disguises the armed robbers were wearing. From witness statements it appears that they were dressed as frogmen, sir.'

'Frog Men?' asked Chapwick, unsure how anyone could sensibly dress up as what were basically humanoid frogs, and still be able to rob a museum.

But thanks to Dewbush clearing his throat beside him, Capstan corrected himself, and instead used the less confusing description of what they were wearing. 'Sorry, I meant scuba divers, sir. Not Frog Men.'

'Ah yes. That does make more sense.'

'So, on Saturday we ran a check on all the shops in the known universe that sell human scuba diving equipment. From that we pulled out a list of all those who'd sold a set matching the description given, and then cross checked that against a list of all known criminals. And after we'd done all that, we came up with a name.'

Chapwick leaned forward in his chair. He was finding the meeting unusually exciting. 'And what name was that?' he asked, secretly hoping that it might be a high ranking politician, or some famous celebrity.

'A Mr Daniel Dumbarton, sir.'

'Daniel Dumbarton?' asked Chapwick. 'I can't say I've ever heard of him.'

'He's a retired restaurant owner who lives in the small coastal town of Padstow, sir.'

'Padstow in the UKA, or the one in the USA?'

'Er, the UKA one, I believe, sir,' replied Capstan, but only because he'd never heard of a Padstow in America. 'He has a criminal record, sir, and so we were hoping you'd give us permission to go there and interview him, possibly with the intention of bringing him back here for questioning.'

'That all sounds very sensible, Capstan,' replied Chapwick, already imagining the media headlines stating that the ring leader for the Final Fish Finger robbery had been apprehended after only two days.

Just as he said that, Capstan's touch-tech watch began playing an upbeat sort of a tune and started glowing blue. Glancing down at it, he saw that the call was from the Forensics Department.

'Would it be OK if I took that, sir? It's Forensics. Hopefully they'll have some news about something we left with them on Saturday.'

'By all means,' said Chapwick, leaning back in his chair.

'Thank you, sir,' said Capstan, and pressed the green button on the side of the watch as he lifted it up towards his mouth.

'Capstan here!'

'Detective Inspector Capstan, we've run that sample you left for us through the computer and it looks like we have a result for you.'

'That's good to hear. And what did you find?'

'The piece of metal we tested used to be a tin of baked beans.'

'A tin of baked beans?' repeated Capstan.

'That's right. More specifically, a tin of Meanz Baked Beans.'

'That is interesting,' said Capstan, but only because the Chief Inspector was sitting opposite, staring at him. He didn't think it was interesting at all, as he really couldn't see how a fragment of metal found inside an explosive device could have any bearing on the case, even if it was from a tin of baked beans.

'We'll send the full report to you along with a holographic image of the object in question.'

'That is most kind of you. Thank you!' said

Capstan, and ended the call.

Curious to know why Forensics had called Capstan about a tin of baked beans, Chapwick asked, 'Another development?'

'Could be, sir,' replied Capstan. 'It's our second line of enquiry, sir. Pieces of shrapnel were found at the museum, after the Fish Finger had been stolen, and we had Forensics run a check to see what one particular piece had been before it was used as shrapnel.'

'How very diligent of you!'

'Thank you, sir.'

'And that object was a tin of Meanz Baked Beans, I take it?' asked Chapwick.

'Apparently it was, sir, but at this stage we'd like to follow up with the first line of enquiry before looking into the tin of baked beans, sir.'

'Yes, well, I think that makes sense, but do keep it in mind, Capstan. In my experience you just never know where an investigation may take you, and it's always worth keeping all doors open. But for now I'd have to agree with you; you should head down to see that chap in Cornwall first.'

'Thank you, sir,' said Capstan. 'We'll leave straight away!'

CHAPTER THIRTEEN

FLYING OVER PADSTOW, Capstan was surprised and delighted to see that it hadn't changed all that much since his day. He'd been there for a week's holiday with his wife, before they'd had children, and although he couldn't recognise anything in particular, it did at least still look like a coastal fishing town, albeit more like one based in Cyprus than on the Cornish Coast. The Mediterranean feel to the place was because all the buildings they could see as Dewbush began their ascent were white with flat roofs, and the whole place shimmered in the heat of what Dewbush seemed to think was just an averagely warm summer's day.

At first, Capstan was also surprised by the fact that there weren't all that many people wondering up and down the streets. In fact, there were probably even less than in his time on Earth, which seemed odd, as the global population had increased exponentially since the beginning of the 21st Century. After giving the matter some consideration, he realised that holidays beside the sea had probably become a thing of the past, as it would be unlikely any right-minded person would want to go anywhere near a beach, and would probably be happier staring at one on a TV monitor, or from a nearby hotel room installed with turbo-charged air-conditioning. But it did at least beg the question as to what people *did* do for their holidays in this day and age, so he decided to ask Dewbush.

'I think most people normally go sightseeing off-planet, sir, although Intergalactic Golf is very popular. And I hear there are some quite excellent ski resorts in the Antarctic, but both are very expensive, and normally the reserve of the rich and famous. Anyway, we're here now, sir,' said Dewbush, as he skilfully landed their unmarked Space Police car on the roof car park of the building that their GPS had guided them to, alongside a red Skoda that Capstan assumed was a flying one, as like every other car he'd so far seen it didn't have any wheels.

Stepping out of the car and into the sweltering inferno of what used to be a major holiday destination, a heat made worse by the fact that they were on the top of the roof of a three-storey building on a cloudless summer's day without so much as a sniff of a breeze, Dewbush said, 'Hopefully someone's in, sir,' as he headed for the steps that led down to the front of the house.

'Hopefully, yes,' agreed Capstan, thinking that if nobody was, then he'd be very tempted to break in simply to get out of the scorching heat.

Once outside the quite charming white wooden front door with its ornate brass door-knocker, and a highly-polished brass letter box with a stained-glassed window above depicting the image of an old gaff-rigged sailing boat, Dewbush rang the bell and then stepped to one side to let Capstan take over.

It wasn't long before the knock was answered by a decrepit old man with beige sagging skin and thinning white hair, who must have been well over three hundred years old and had either run out of money or lost interest in having new hair and skin to keep him looking a little more youthful, like most other people seemed to.

'Mr Daniel Dumbarton?' asked Capstan, as he retrieved his Space Police ID from his inside suit jacket pocket.

'Who wants to know?'

'I'm Detective Inspector Capstan and this is my colleague, Lieutenant Dewbush. We're from the UKA Space Police.'

'Space Police, eh?' asked the old man, as he leaned forward to study the two IDs. 'And what did you say your names were again?'

'Detective Inspector Capstan and Lieutenant Dewbush.'

'That one says "Detective Inspector Cat*spam*",' said the old man, pointing at Capstan's.

It was odd. Back in his day, nobody ever seemed to give his police ID a second look, but now an intricate study of it seemed almost mandatory.

'Yes, well, unfortunately it's spelt wrong. It should say Capstan.'

'So which one is it then, Capstan or Catspam?'

'It's Capstan,' said Capstan. 'Would it be possible for us to come in?' he asked, keen to get out of the oppressive summer heat and even more so to get off the subject of his miss-spelt surname.

'You'd better, I suppose. Besides, you wouldn't last long out there. Not in those suits,' and he led the way inside what to Capstan's relief was a cool, fully air-conditioned home, with a faint smell of recently deceased old people, a bit like a 21st Century charity shop.

'So what's this all about then?' asked the old man, as he walked into his sitting room.

Deciding to jump straight in, Capstan said, 'We understand you've recently bought some scuba diving gear.'

'That's right. What of it?'

'And that you not only bought one set, but five?'

'Yes, yes. Five sets. Why, is it suddenly against the law to buy more than one of something?'

'So you're not denying it then?'

'So it is against the law then?' he sighed, but was hardly surprised. Everything changed so quickly these days that it was becoming increasingly difficult for him to keep up.

'Er, not that I know of,' answered Capstan, looking

around at Dewbush for guidance on that one. Seeing Dewbush shake his head, Capstan went on, 'I suppose it depends on what you intended to use them for,' thinking that made quite a good question.

'Well, I only needed one set for myself. The others were for my friends.'

'Ahhh haaa!' cried Capstan, as if he'd just managed to single-handedly solve the entire case.

'That's right,' Dumbarton continued. 'I've started a little scuba diving club with my friends from the bar.'

'A little scuba diving club?' repeated Capstan.

'That's what I said, yes. Why?'

'And where do you do this so-called "scuba diving"?'

'On top of Mount Kilimanjaro. Where do you think?' answered the old man, clearly becoming a little irritated.

'He's lying, sir,' said Dewbush. 'You'd need climbing gear to get to the top of Mount Kilimanjaro.'

'I suspect he was joking, Dewbush,' said Capstan.

'Is that correct, Mr Dumbarton?' asked Dewbush, in a clear tone of accusatory disapproval. 'Were you telling a joke?'

The old man didn't like the sound of that. He'd forgotten that the telling of jokes had become a criminal offence, and back-pedalled as best he could, saying, 'Not at all. The air at the top of Mount Kilimanjaro is very thin. It's also quite cold, I believe, so I'd have thought the wearing of scuba diving equipment would have made both a sensible and practical choice.'

'He has a point, sir,' said Dewbush, glancing over at Capstan. 'It's very possible that he did buy it to climb Mount Kilimanjaro.'

Capstan turned to stare back at his lieutenant. If there was one thing he really didn't like about this new century he'd found himself living in, it was that some complete moron had come up with the idea that that the telling of jokes should be made illegal, and had then decided to include what he considered to be its most useful form, that of sarcasm.

'Anyway,' said Capstan, keen to stay as far away from the subject of illegal joke-telling as possible, 'may I ask what you were doing on Saturday, at around lunchtime?'

'On Saturday?'

'That's right, at around half one in the afternoon?'

'And what day is it today?'

'It's Monday.'

'Right, yes of course it is. So, if it's Monday today, then Saturday must have been the day before yesterday,' he continued, now staring up at the ceiling, 'which means that it was have been…er…two days ago. Yes, that's right. Not yesterday but the day before would be two days ago. So what was I doing two days ago, on what must have been Saturday?'

105

'That's what we're trying to ascertain, Mr Dumbarton,' said Capstan, trying to be as patient as possible.

'What time on Saturday did you say again?'

'At around half one in the afternoon.'

'So lunchtime then?'

'That's right, Mr Dumbarton. Saturday afternoon at around half one, which could correctly be referred to as lunchtime.'

'Right.' He gazed up at the ceiling again for a few moments. 'I'm sorry, I just can't remember. I'm going to have to look it up in my diary.' With that, he set off to hobble around his flat, peering around the place as he did so.

'I don't suppose anyone's seen my PalmPad?' he asked. 'I'm sure your eyes are better than mine.'

'I think it's here, Mr Dumbarton,' said Capstan, retrieving it from the top of an antique-looking dark wood coffee table. Lying beside it was an actual real-life copy of the Radio Times, which prompted him to say, 'I'm surprised they still print this!' as he picked that up as well to have a quick flick through.

'Oh, yes. My wife had a subscription through YouGet, and I've just never gotten around to cancelling it.'

'I assume your wife's no longer with us?' asked Capstan, beginning to take a more empathetic approach to his questioning. He knew the feeling of recent personal loss all too well.

'I'm afraid not,' said the old man. 'She ran off with my neighbour last year.'

'Oh, I see,' said Capstan, unsure how such an ancient-looking man's wife would be able to run anywhere, but then thought that she must have spent more money on body part upgrades than he had, and maybe that had been the problem with the marriage. Or alternatively that he'd simply married someone a lot younger than himself. But obviously none of that was pertinent to his current line of enquiry, so he handed the old man his PalmPad so that he'd be able to admit that he was indeed robbing the British Museum with his friends on Saturday, dressed up in the scuba diving outfits, but had somehow managed to forget about it.

'Oh yes, of course!' continued the old man, once he'd accessed his PalmPad's calendar app. 'I'd popped round to see my mum that day.'

'Your mum?' asked Capstan, wondering if anyone on planet Earth ever died anymore.

'That's right. She only lives down the road.'

'Right, well, may we at least see the scuba diving gear you bought?'

'Of course. It's just through here,' and he doddered off back into the hallway.

As soon as he was out of earshot, Capstan said to Dewbush, 'You go with him and keep him busy looking at his scuba diving gear, whilst I search his kitchen for the Fish Finger.'

'Good idea, sir,' answered Dewbush, and followed the old man out.

About ten minutes later, Dewbush returned to the sitting room with the old man carrying a pair of bright yellow flippers, a navy blue full-length wetsuit and a diver's mask. As he entered, he saw Capstan standing in the middle of the room doing his best not to look as if he'd just been searching through the suspect's entire kitchen in a desperate and wholly unauthorised search for the Final Fish Finger.

'Did you find anything, sir?' whispered Dewbush to him as he came back in.

'Not a sausage,' replied Capstan.

'Oh, right. But, aren't we looking for a Fish Finger, sir?'

'Yes, of course we are, Dewbush.'

'But you just said you couldn't find a sausage.'

'It's just an expression, Dewbush.'

'Oh, I see. So, you didn't find a sausage then?'

'No, of course I didn't find a sausage!'

'What about the Fish Finger, sir?'

Capstan sighed. 'I didn't find that either, Dewbush.'

'Do you think it would be worth me having a look, sir?' asked Dewbush, still unsure as to if his boss had been looking for a sausage or the fish finger they were supposed to be searching for.

'You may as well, Dewbush,' replied Capstan. 'Tell you what, if I chat to him about the Radio Times, then you can sneak out when he's not looking.'

Unfortunately, despite their very best efforts, neither of them were able to find any evidence of either the Final Fish Finger or a sausage; and when they checked up with the old people's home where he said he had been on Saturday afternoon, at around lunchtime, the staff confirmed it.

So crossing Mr Dumbarton off their list of potential suspects, they made their way back up on to the roof and into their car, where Dewbush asked, 'What now, sir?'

'Well, Dewbush, I suppose we don't have any choice but to follow our other line of enquiry.'

'You mean, the tin of baked beans, sir?'

'That's the one, Dewbush, yes!'

CHAPTER FOURTEEN

USING HIS PALMPAD, Dewbush pulled up the 3D image of the tin of baked beans that Forensics had sent over for Capstan and himself to take a closer look at. And having rotated the holographic image above his phone a few times, Dewbush said, 'It just looks like a normal tin of baked beans, sir.'

Capstan also peered at it. 'I think there's more we can derive from it, Dewbush. Firstly, it's not *just* a tin of baked beans, it's a tin of *Meanz* Baked Beans!'

'Yes, sir, of course,' said Dewbush, although he'd no idea what difference that made, but having to assume his boss had a reason to think that it was relevant, somehow, he thought it would help if he told his boss about how it was advertised, and sang out. 'MEANZ MEANS BEANS!'

'Do you *still* have that ad?' asked Capstan, remembering one particular time when he was about five years old, sitting in front of the TV inside his childhood home watching that very advert whilst playing with his Lego.

'Of course, sir. Why? Did you have the same one?'

'Believe it or not, we did, Dewbush, but I can't say I'm too surprised. I always thought it was a good ad.'

'To be honest, sir, I'm struggling to see how all this is connected to the Case of the Final Fish Finger,' admitted Dewbush.

Capstan wasn't sure either, but was trying to think outside the box as best he could, or at least outside the tin of baked beans that he was still staring at. But it wasn't working, so he thought he'd take a break from trying to think outside the tin and have a go at thinking inside it instead.

'Is there anything that says where the baked beans were made?'

'There is, sir, yes,' and after examining the small print on the back of the label, said, 'They're made in China, sir.'

'China!' exclaimed Capstan.

'Yes, sir. But everything's made in China these days.'

A momentary paused followed as Capstan digested that piece of information, before Dewbush asked, 'Do you think we should go there, sir, to have a look around?'

'To China?' asked Capstan.

'Yes, sir. There's a postcode on the tin, and it wouldn't take us long.'

'I suppose it wouldn't,' mused Capstan, who was beginning to get used to the idea that it was now possible to travel unimaginably vast distances in relatively short periods of time. So, with them both thinking that they should make the trip, Dewbush punched the postcode into the car's GPS; and after putting their seatbelts on, they set off for the other side of the planet.

CHAPTER FIFTEEN

ABOUT FORTY-FIVE minutes later, they reached the outskirts of a town called Jiaxing located to the west of Shanghai, in China.

As they slowly descended to land in a car park within a very normal-looking industrial estate, Capstan asked Dewbush, 'How's your Chinese?'

'How's my what, sir?'

'Your Chinese, Dewbush? I assume you don't speak it.'

'Er…I'm not sure what you mean, sir?'

'I assume you don't speak Chinese, Dewbush. Or do you?'

It was only then that Dewbush understood what he'd meant as he remembered what he'd learnt about at school; that in the olden days all the countries of Earth spoke different languages.

'I see what you mean, sir. No, sir. Unfortunately I don't speak Chinese, but I'm not sure that anyone does anymore. It was back when America took over the world that English became the official language of Earth, and all the other ones gradually died out.'

'So, everyone speaks English now, do they?' asked Capstan, thinking that it was just about the most sensible thing he'd heard since he'd been defrosted.

'Yes, sir,' confirmed Dewbush. 'My teacher told us that it was a very difficult time for both business and tourism when everyone spoke different languages.'

'Your teacher was right, Dewbush, it was! But I'm pleased to learn that everyone saw sense in the end.'

As Dewbush eased the car down, he looked ahead and said, 'There's a sign for the Meanz Baked Beans factory just up ahead, sir. But I suggest we tread carefully when we go in, though. We don't have jurisdiction for the United Asia of America, sir, and we'd have to get a warrant before either searching the premises or taking anyone in for questioning.'

'I understand, Dewbush, but I only want to have a look around. If we see anything suspicious, we can always get a warrant and come back.'

'Right you are, sir!'

With that, Dewbush stepped out, and Capstan followed him, straight into what felt like a solid wall of heat that was almost impossible to walk in, let alone breathe, and his first step faltered as he felt the air burning the inside of his nostrils. Feeling his human leg give way, he reached for the car's bonnet to stop himself from falling over, but that was so hot that it burnt his hand, forcing him to stand up straight again.

'Is your leg all right, sir?' asked Dewbush, assuming that it must be running out of batteries.

'The leg's fine, Dewbush, but I'm not sure about my hand.'

'Why's that, sir?'

'Never mind, Dewbush,' said Capstan, as he examined it.

Relieved to see that it hadn't burnt after all, he stared over at his subordinate who didn't seem fazed by the extraordinary temperature in the slightest.

'How can you stand it, Dewbush?'

'Stand what, sir?'

'The heat!'

Looking around, Dewbush said, 'I suppose it is a little warmer than the UKA, sir, but I'm sure you'll get used to it.'

'That's what you told me last time.'

'I know, sir. But that was only last week. It will probably take you a month or two.'

'Let's get inside, shall we?' suggested Capstan, still clutching at his hand. 'Before my brain melts!'

'Don't worry, sir,' said Dewbush, following him. 'It's not hot enough for your brain to melt. That sort of thing only happens nearer the Equator.'

As they marched towards a doorway set in a large corrugated iron factory, above which a sign said "Reception", Capstan realised Dewbush couldn't have been joking. 'Remind me not to go anywhere near the Equator, then! At least not without a wide-brimmed hat.'

'That's not a bad idea, sir,' said Dewbush. 'I'm sure you could get one of those from YouGet.'

Thinking it probably best not to tell Dewbush that he'd already bought one from YouGet, along with numerous other items, none of which he'd actually wanted, he was first to reach the door. Relieved to find it open, as the sign in the window had suggested, he walked straight in to a refreshingly cool reception area that must have been temperature controlled by a supercomputer linked up to some sort of nuclear powered air-conditioning system.

Seeing the reception desk over to the left, Capstan pulled out his ID and, after giving the stunningly attractive beige-skinned girl sitting behind the desk the briefest of glances at it, so that she didn't notice that it only covered the UKA, and also so that she didn't have a chance to see how his name had been spelt, said, 'Space Police! Is it all right if we take a look around?'

'Oh! Er, hello. Um, I'm not sure, really,' she said. 'Have we done anything wrong?'

'Not yet,' said Capstan.

'Right, well, I'll see if I can find Mr Wong for you. He's the factory manager.'

She leaned forward and said, 'Mr Wong to reception. Mr Wong to reception,' and they heard the message echo out beyond the room they were in. Then she looked over at the two Space Policemen and said, 'If you would take a seat, I'm sure he won't be long.'

A few minutes later, after Capstan and Dewbush

had sat down and had a couple of glasses of water each from the water cooler, a very beige-looking man with sandy brown hair, who to Capstan's eyes looked no more Chinese than a Safebusy's stir fry ready meal, came in through a small side door.

'Mr Wong,' said the receptionist. 'These men are from Space Police,' and she gestured over at the two men in question.

As soon as Capstan realised it was the man whom the receptionist had called for, he stood up. 'I'm Detective Inspector Capstan and this here is Lieutenant Dewbush. We were just wondering if we could have a very quick look around?'

'We haven't done anything wrong, have we?' asked the man, which Capstan thought was odd, being that's exactly what the receptionist had asked.

'Nothing yet, Mr Wong, no. But if we *could* have a look around, that would be appreciated.'

'I see,' said Mr Wong, before asking, 'and I take it you have a search warrant?'

'Er, no, we don't, but in fairness we don't need one, as we're not conducting a search of the premises. We'd simply like to look inside it.'

'And the difference between you looking inside it and searching the premises is...?'

The combination of the man's reluctance for them to have a look around and the fact that both he and the receptionist had asked if they'd done anything wrong for no particular reason was beginning to ring alarm bells for Capstan, or at least a solitary police siren; but this only served to make Capstan more determined to take a look inside. 'The difference is, Mr Wong, that looking around only involves using the eyes, hence the reason for it being called "looking around", whereas searching involves lifting things up to look underneath them. We only need a warrant to do the latter, but we're well within our rights to do the former, as long as we don't touch anything whilst we're doing it.'

Capstan had no idea if that was true, but it sounded good.

'Well, I'd love to let you have a look around,' began Mr Wong, 'but unfortunately we're closed for, er, for…maintenance, so if you could come back another day, that would be great,' and he motioned for them to leave.

'You're closed, are you?' asked Capstan.

'That's right. Sorry about that. So if you could just pop yourselves outside, that would be appreciated.'

'But the sign on the door said you're open.'

'Yes, well, I must have turned it over by accident when I arrived this morning.'

'And your receptionist didn't say anything about you being closed when we came in.'

'Ah, well, yes. But she's, er, new.'

'And the fact that's she's in, sitting behind

reception, would also suggest that you're open, wouldn't it?'

'It may look that way, but she only came in for her…induction. Isn't that right, Miss Wang?'

'That's right, Mr Wong. I just popped in to learn how to use the, er… intercom system!' and she gave Capstan a rather good version of a completely innocent smile.

But Capstan wasn't convinced, not by a long way, and he looked back at the factory manager. 'What is it, exactly, that you're trying to hide, Mr Wong?'

'Hide? Why do you think we're trying to hide anything?'

'Just call it a hunch.'

'Call it a what?'

'A hunch, Mr Wong.'

'I'm sorry, Detective, but I can't say I've ever heard of a hunch before. Is it something you have between breakfast and lunch?'

'Never mind that. I'd like to see inside your factory. If not, we'll be heading back to the car to call for a warrant. That should take us about twenty seconds. And about five minutes later our entire Forensics Department will be descending onto your factory to start pulling the building apart.'

'All right, all right,' capitulated Mr Wong, deciding that it would probably be best if he just let them in. He led them over towards the door he'd just come through, saying, 'You can come in, but I can assure you that there's absolutely nothing illegal going on here.'

Stepping through the door, Capstan and Dewbush were greeted by a vast warehouse stacked to the ceiling with what must be thousands upon thousands of tins of baked beans.

'As you can see,' continued Mr Wong, gesticulating up at the line after line of shelving, 'we have nothing to hide.'

'And can we see where you actually make the baked beans?'

'Ah, well, to be completely honest with you, Detective, we don't actually make them here anymore.'

'But doesn't it say that you do on the tin?'

'Well, yes. And we used to. But when we were bought out, the new owner decided that it would be cheaper to move production off-planet, and to use the factory purely for storage.'

At this point, Dewbush stepped in.

'So why does it still say on your tins that they're made in China?'

'Um, well, because we were concerned that if we told people they weren't anymore, then it could have an adverse effect on sales. However, I'm one-hundred percent sure that that's not illegal though.'

'Maybe not, Mr Wong,' continued Dewbush, who really didn't like companies who used any sort of misleading advertising, 'but it's not right though, is it? In fact, I'd almost definitely say that it was wrong. It's not right that you don't make them here when you say you do, and it's not right that you haven't told anyone. And although it may not be against the law, two wongs don't make a right, do they, Mr Wrong?' said Dewbush, pleased to have concluded that little lecture as he could feel himself becoming increasingly confused as to exactly who was right and who was Mr Wong.

'So, where are they made now?' asked Capstan, who didn't care about the difference between right and wrong, but simply wanted to push forward with the case, and at the moment they were getting nowhere.

'It's the new owner's home planet, called Ganymede. It's one of Jupiter's moons; the largest one, in fact.'

'And does the owner have a name?'

'Mr Obadiah. Gorgnome Obadiah.'

'OK, but we're going to need his address as well.'

'I'm sure that would be OK.' Turning to the receptionist, he said, 'Miss Wang, could you please provide these gentlemen with Mr Obadiah's contact details?'

CHAPTER SIXTEEN

HAVING SETTLED himself back in the White House with his wife-bot, Susan, and after a pleasant Sunday afternoon playing Intergalactic Golf with his son – he couldn't remember which one, but it was definitely one of them – it was now Monday morning, and President Müller was back behind his desk in the Oval Office feeling slightly better about the world after the tediously dull Intergalactic Trade Talks he'd attended in London.

In fairness, the summit hadn't been that bad. OK, it had, but the last part he'd actually really enjoyed. That was when he'd launched a full-frontal attack against seven thousand fish-eating protestors armed only with a 7 iron. And he'd been able to share the experience with Susan, who'd decided to join him with a sand wedge. Beating up a disgruntled bunch of left-wing socialists had proven to be remarkably good therapy. Not only that, it had also strengthened the relationship he had with his robot wife, who he now saw in a completely new light and had subsequently decided to propose to, at some point at least. Furthermore, he was convinced that it had also improved his golf swing, which had been demonstrably proven the day before as he'd beaten his son by over three shots, something he hadn't done in a very long time.

Unfortunately, just as he'd started the second level of what was turning out to be a very exciting first-person shooter game called Zombies Warmed Up on his desk-sized touch-tech device, his Chief of Staff, Gavin Sherburt, walked in, presumably to go over the day's itinerary.

'Good morning, Mr President, and how was the rest of your weekend?' he asked, as he approached the Oval Office's desk.

After a quick glance up, Müller said, 'Completely ruined for having to see you again, thank you, Gavin.'

Knowing that his Commander-in-Chief was always a little grumpy on a Monday morning, Gavin was able to shrug off the derogatory remark like oil off a robot's back and to ask with a cheerful tone, 'Were you able to play golf with David as you'd hoped?'

'David! That's what his name was! I really couldn't remember. I kept calling him "Son" all the time.' Looking up again, Müller asked, 'He was my son, wasn't he?'

'David is one of them, yes, Mr President. From your twenty-third marriage, I believe.'

'Well anyway, I beat him, which is always good.'

Hoping that his Commander-in-Chief's spirits had been lifted after being reminded about his game of golf, Gavin asked, 'Would you like to go over the day's itinerary now, Mr President?'

'You know I wouldn't, Gavin, thank you.'

'It will only take five minutes, Mr President.'

'The fact that it will take any time at all is bad enough, but knowing that it will lead straight in to another day of boring and predominately pointless meetings will simply make it worse. And anyway, after what I had to put up with on Saturday, I'd have thought you'd have given me the day off!'

'I fully understand how you must feel, Mr President.'

'Do you, Gavin?'

'Well…'

'So you're saying that you know what it's like to be the President of Earth, are you?'

'I, er…'

'And that you understand the intense pressure I'm under, every single day?'

'Um…'

'And that I literally have the whole world resting on my shoulders?'

'Well, no, Mr President, I couldn't possibly know how it must feel, but I hope to at least try to be able to understand the many challenges you must have to face,' responded Gavin, thinking that if the guy didn't like the job, then he should quit. God knows he'd been doing it for long enough.

Still seeing Gavin hovering in front of his desk like a levitating Buddhist Monk who'd ditched the saffron robe in exchange for a tailor-made business suit, and knowing that it was highly unlikely that he'd budge before going over his itinerary, Müller let out a heavy sigh. And glancing down to see that he was in the process of being eaten by a particularly unattractive zombie, he gave up with the computer game, sat back in his chair, and said, 'Go on then. What enthralling meetings have you lined up for me today?'

Before he changed his mind, Gavin launched straight into it.

'At ten o'clock, Mr President, you have a meeting with the ITU…'

'What, *again*!'

Gavin had been expecting that.

'Regrettably, yes, Mr President. The decision made to ban fishing would appear to be having some rather unexpected repercussions around the world which they'd like to discuss with you.'

'I don't see how that's suddenly become my problem. They're the ones who voted to ban it, not me!'

'I know, Mr President, but unfortunately that's the decision that was made, and now they need to find a way to make it work.'

'I'd have thought the solution was obvious, Gavin. To take another vote on it but for them to heed my advice this time.'

'I'm not sure that would help, Mr President, even if

they were to agree.'

'And why's that, Gavin? Do tell!'

'It's the latest global fish stock report, Mr President. It was published this morning, and the situation is looking far worse than anyone had expected. I have it here, if you'd like to read it?'

'I really wouldn't, thank you.'

'OK, well, to summarise the report's findings, basically all forms of white fish have now been officially classified as endangered species, and as some haven't been reported as being caught in over four weeks, it may be that a number of them have already become extinct.'

'That's a shame, but it just means what I've been saying all along; that we're going to have to push down the route of Biological Digital Printing, aren't we?'

'Yes, Mr President, but unfortunately a report's come in about that as well. It states that the scientific community has reached a bit of an impasse with regards to making progress, and they've put the expected time for effective biological digital printing back by five years, maybe more.'

'Five years?'

'That's what it says, Mr President.'

'Then we have no choice. We'll just have to increase their budget.'

'Unfortunately, Mr President, they're saying that a cash injection wouldn't make a huge amount of difference at this stage. The report's executive summary says that the process of being able to reproduce complex living biological organisms using a printer is far more problematical than they'd first thought. They now think that they're going to have to develop a whole new generation of computers first, before being able to handle the amount of data necessary to do it. And meanwhile, protests have broken out in every major city around the world, which, combined with a general Earth-wide strike in response to how the planet's fishermen have been treated, has sent the stock market into freefall and there have been calls on this morning's news that there should be another election, Mr President.'

That last nugget of information was enough for Müller to begin to take the matter a little more seriously. He'd not heard the word election used in a conversation for many, many years. In fact, he couldn't even remember the last time he'd heard the word spoken, or even seen it featured in the news.

'But the last report I saw said that they'd be able to start printing out fish within a matter of months, not years!'

'I know, Mr President. It's a most unfortunate delay.'

'And what happened to all the fish anyway? They told me at the weekend that there was enough for at least two years, maybe even three.'

'Nobody seems to know, Mr President. The current thinking at the moment is that the computer model used to calculate how many fish were left was running on Doorway 10, when it should have been upgraded to Doorway 12 before running the analysis. Either that, or someone's been sucking the fish out of the ocean without anyone noticing.'

'Is that likely?' asked Müller.

'I shouldn't have thought so, Mr President.'

There was a pause in their conversation, before Müller asked, 'And is the ITU putting forward a solution, or are they expecting me to come up with the answer as they normally do?'

'Well, Mr President, they've been sent a proposal from Mr Obadiah.'

'Who?'

'Mr Obadiah, Mr President. He was that lifeform you had that meeting with on Saturday morning, the one with the big hands and large yellow feet.'

'You mean the one who'd smelt like a rotting dead fish floating at the bottom of a toilet and who tried to play me by offering to sell me fish at what I seem to remember was ten times the going rate?'

'That's the one, Mr President, yes, although he's since brought down his offer to only five times the current rate, on the condition that you sign a ten year contract with him and buy more than a hundred billion fish in the first six months.'

'A hundred billion fish?'

'That's right, Mr President, although that's probably about the level we'd need to meet current demand.'

'My God! Do we really get through that many fish?'

'At least that, Mr President, yes.'

'But could we even afford to buy that many, and at that price?'

'We'd have to cut our defence budget, but yes, it's possible.'

Müller stood up and began walking up and down behind his desk. He really didn't like the Obadiah creature, and the mere idea of having to agree to his terms made him fume with indignation.

About a minute later, after he'd been pacing up and down the carpet like an over-achieving lawnmower, he eventually said, 'Is there really no other choice?'

'I think that's what the ITU would like to talk to you about, Mr President, but at the moment it doesn't look like there is, no.'

Resuming his seat behind his desk, Müller said, 'Unfortunately Gavin, I'm going to need an option two. So if you can't provide me with one, then I guess I'm going to have to come up with one all on my own.'

'And the meeting with the ITU?'

'Postpone it till tomorrow, and I'll ask the wife tonight to see what she thinks.'

CHAPTER SEVENTEEN

AFTER THE RECEPTIONIST at the Meanz baked bean factory had given them the owner's address, Capstan and Dewbush left the premises, raced back to their car to get out of the heat as quickly as possible, inputted their new destination's postcode and, after putting their seat belts on and turning the air-conditioning up to full, set off: destination Ganymede, just next door to Jupiter. It was only then that Dewbush remembered their Chief Inspector, and that they'd probably better send an interim report over to him before they left.

'Is that really necessary?' asked Capstan, who'd never been one for writing reports, let alone interim ones.

'It's either that or we phone him up, sir,' said Dewbush. 'It's one thing going to China, but Ganymede is over three-hundred and ninety million miles away, and we're going to have to justify both the time and the fuel expenditure. And also, once we get there we won't be able to phone him until we get back, and he'll begin to wonder where we've got to.'

'Fair enough, but I'm not writing a report. What's his phone number?'

'It'll be on your phone, sir.'

'You mean my watch?'

'That's the one. If you just say "Chief Inspector Chapwick" into it whilst pressing the green button, that should dial his number.'

Moments later, Capstan heard the Chief Inspector's rather curt response to having been phoned up by someone, which was simply, 'Chapwick!'

'Hello, sir, it's Detective Inspector Capstan here.'

'Ah, Capstan. I've been meaning to call you. How's the case going, or should I say the cases?'

'Unfortunately, sir, the lead we had in Padstow proved to be a bit of a dead end.'

'Oh really? How come?'

'The suspect was just an old man who'd bought the flippers and the wetsuits to set up a scuba diving club with his friends. And we had a good poke around his kitchen but couldn't find any evidence of the Final Fish Finger.'

'I see,' said Chapwick. 'Did you look in the freezer?'

'We both did, sir, yes.'

'And what about the top compartment of the fridge?'

'There as well, sir. But there was no sign of it.'

'Well, I suppose he could've eaten it. Did he have any tins of baked beans and tomato ketchup lying around?'

'Not that we saw, sir, no. We also checked out his alibi, and he was with his mum at the time of the robbery, as he said he was.'

'That's a shame. So, what's your next step?'

'We decided to follow our second line of investigation, sir; that of the fragment of metal found at the museum. After analysing the holographic image of the tin it originated from, we found out that it was made in China, sir.'

'China!'

'Yes, sir, although apparently everything's made in China these days. So anyway, we popped over there and discovered that they're not made there any more, as the business was recently bought out by some chap called…'

Capstan couldn't remember his name, and signalled Dewbush for help, prompting the lieutenant to lean over and whisper, 'Gorgnome Obadiah,' into Capstan's ear.

'Gorgnome Obadiah, sir,' continued Capstan, 'who moved production of the actual baked beans to his home planet.'

'And which planet is that?' asked Chapwick.

'Ganymede, sir.'

'Ganymede?'

'Yes, sir, although apparently it's not classed as a planet, but a large moon that orbits Jupiter.'

'And you'd like permission to go there, I assume?'

'We would, sir, yes.'

'OK, well, I suppose you'd better. At least it's closer

than Titan. But if it turns out to be another dead end, I'd like you back here as soon as you can. Unfortunately, another fleet of fishing trawlers has been reported going missing from the North Sea.'

'Another one, sir?'

'Apparently, yes. So if there are no other leads for the stolen Fish Finger, I'd like you back on that case, and perhaps you could charter a boat and have a bit of a look around for them.'

'You'd like us to look for the fleet of missing fishing trawlers...in the North Sea, sir?'

'I know it's not ideal, Capstan, but with no other leads to go on, at least it would be a start.'

'Yes, of course, sir. But is there nobody else who could take a look for them, sir? Perhaps someone with a little more sea experience?'

Capstan did have some experience of going to sea, but only in the Solent and the English Channel, and he really didn't fancy a boating trip anywhere near the North one.

'Under normal circumstances I probably would, Capstan, but the weekend's worldwide ban on fishing has sparked a fair amount of civil unrest, and we're having to cope with riots breaking out in just about every major city in the UKA.'

'I see, sir. Well, we'll take a look at this baked bean factory on Ganymede, but if it doesn't lead anywhere then we'll head straight back and have a look for those fishing boats, sir.'

'That's the spirit, Capstan. Give me a call when you get back, and good luck!'

'Thank you, sir.'

With the call ended, with some apprehension, Dewbush asked, 'Are we really going to charter a boat and go to the North Sea?' Since he'd spoken to Capstan about it earlier, Dewbush had done a Dongle search and had found out it was considerably larger than he'd previously thought, and had subsequently changed his mind about wanting to go anywhere near the place.

'Hopefully we won't have to, Dewbush. I can't help but think that the two cases are related, somehow. The connection with fish is just too big a coincidence. Let's just hope we can find some answers on Ganymede.'

'But if we can't, sir, then how are we going to look for fishing trawlers in the North Sea?'

'At this stage, Dewbush, I've no idea, but there's probably a return ferry to Norway we can take that would at least allow us to say that we'd had a go.'

CHAPTER EIGHTEEN

A S IT TURNED OUT, Chapwick was right. Ganymede was a fair bit closer than Titan. This meant that as their unmarked Space Police car travelled at light speed towards their destination, Capstan and Dewbush were only able to get a couple of hours' sleep in before reaching the most significant of Jupiter's moons and the ninth largest object in the whole of the solar system.

As the GPS announced that they would need to turn left in a hundred thousand miles, they both yawned and stretched themselves out as best they could within the front seats of their car, after which they put their seats back into an upright position. Once done, Dewbush disengaged the autopilot to begin slowing the car down to a more sensible speed for their final approach.

'So what's this Ganymede place like?' asked Capstan, not only to make conversation but also to make sure he didn't step out of the car when they got there to be instantly killed by some highly toxic atmosphere that Dewbush had neglected to mention.

'I've never been, sir. I don't think humans go there very often. It's certainly not one of the main intergalactic holiday hotspots.'

'Do you at least know if it has an atmosphere?'

'Apparently it does, sir, yes, although it doesn't contain enough oxygen for a human to breathe. Although saying that, I heard somewhere that they've been doing a fair amount of terraforming over the last couple of decades, so that may have changed.'

'What about gravity?' asked Capstan, who was equally as keen not to float off into space as he was not to die of asphyxiation.

'Apparently it's similar to that of Earth's moon, sir. Slightly more so than Titan's, but still not enough for us to walk on.'

'So it's air helmets and gravity-coats again then?' asked Capstan, adding a sigh onto the end to signify his general displeasure at having to wear either.

'I think so, sir, yes, although it should at least be warmer than Titan, as it's nearer the sun, so we probably won't have to keep the coats done up.'

'And is there anything else I should know about before we land?' asked Capstan. 'Roaming herds of Tyrannosaurus Rex, for example? Or maybe spiders the size of a football pitch, or huge great worm-like creatures with ten rows of teeth and platoons of armed locals riding on their backs?'

'Apart from the radiation, sir, I don't think so, no.'

'Apart from the radiation?' repeated Capstan, turning to stare at him.

'Yes, sir, but don't worry. Our suits are lined with

136

Radion.'

'And that's supposed to protect us from radiation, is it?'

'Radion is a manmade material that provides radiological protection, sir. It's been sewn into the lining of our suits. Our gravity-coats have it as well, sir, so I can't see that the radiation will be a problem.'

'That's OK then,' said Capstan, thinking that it didn't sound OK at all. However, he didn't think he had any choice other than to trust his subordinate, but would make sure to let him get out of the car first so that he could see if he turned green and keeled over before being set upon by some sort of mutated cross between Godzilla and a hamster.

'We're beginning our descent, sir,' said Dewbush, now fully engrossed in the task of landing their Space Police car without putting a dent in it.

'It looks awfully wet down there,' said Capstan, staring down at a planet that seemed to be covered in nothing more than a seemingly endless expanse of ocean.

'Doesn't it, sir,' agreed Dewbush, gazing around for somewhere even vaguely suitable to set the car down.

'Almost as if there wasn't any land at all,' added Capstan. 'Are you sure this is the right planet?'

It was a good question, and Dewbush decided he'd better check his GPS navigation system.

'It says it is, sir, yes. The external environmental

sensors are also detecting that there's more oxygen than we first thought. A similar amount as Earth's, in fact.'

'Well, I can't see any sign of a baked bean factory, Dewbush,' said Capstan. 'To be honest, I can't see signs of any sort of a factory, or even the land that a factory could be built on. They must have given us the wrong address.'

'You could be right there, sir,' agreed Dewbush, and after flying around in a big circle, with neither one of them seeing anything other than a vast ocean that continued to stretch out beneath them as far as the eye could see, he eventually asked, 'What do you think we should do, sir?'

'I don't know, but we can't just fly around like this all day.'

'Maybe we could ask someone if they know where the baked bean factory is, sir.'

'Great idea, Dewbush – or at least it would be if we could see anyone to ask.'

'Tell you what, sir. I'll turn the thermal imaging camera on. That will at least help us to locate any warm-blooded lifeform who may be down there.'

A push of a button later and Capstan and Dewbush were staring at the dashboard's touch-tech screen that, instead of showing a map, now presented a thermal image depicting a wide variety of green and blue shaped blobs.

After about a minute or so of staring at it, and having seen nothing even closely resembling the shape of a lifeform who might know where the baked bean factory was, Capstan asked, 'What exactly am I looking for, Dewbush?'

'Areas of orange or red should depict living organisms, sir. The bigger the area, the larger the lifeform. However, if it's really big, then it's probably more likely to be a volcano.'

'And what are all those green patterns that look as if they're swirling around in giant circles?'

'To be honest, sir, I'm not sure.'

'Look!' exclaimed Capstan. 'I think there's one there! In the right hand corner,' and he pointed at the screen where there was indeed a red blob, albeit a very small one.

'It's not very big, sir.'

'Beggars can't be choosers, Dewbush.'

'Beggars can't be what, sir?'

'Beggars can't be choosers, Dewbush. It means that as it's the only red blob there, I suggest we take a look.'

'And that's what "beggars can't be choosers" means, is it sir?'

'No, Dewbush. It means that we don't exactly have a vast selection of red blobs to choose from, so either we take a look to see what that one is, or we continue to fly around until we run out of petrol, ditch into the sea and drown.'

Still confused as to what the phrase "Beggars can't be choosers" meant, Dewbush decided that it would probably be better to look it up on Dongle later than to ask his boss again. So for now he simply said, 'Right you are, sir,' and steered their car over to starboard until the red dot was at the top of the screen so that they could begin flying over towards it.

CHAPTER NINETEEN

A S THE SPACE POLICE car raced over the ocean in the direction of the red blob that was still displayed on the car's thermal imaging screen, it wasn't long before Dewbush, staring straight ahead, spotted something, and pointed it out to Capstan. 'Can you see that, sir?'

Sitting forward in his passenger seat, Capstan peered out through the windscreen, but his eyesight couldn't have been as good as Dewbush's as all he could see was a never-ending expanse of undulating ocean.

As the object grew larger, Dewbush said, 'It looks like some sort of a sailing boat, sir.'

By then Capstan could see it, and once they'd drawn a little closer he said, 'It looks more like a dinghy,' and he was right. Coming up fast was a small wooden sailing boat with two bright red sails. As it bounced over the waves looking like a toddler let loose inside a shop that sold both beds and mattresses, they saw that at the helm appeared to be a small boy wearing a navy blue wetsuit, a black diver's mask and bright red flippers, who looked as if he was having a whale of a time.

Moments later, the boy spotted them, and taking

hold of the boat's tiller and mainsheet in one hand, started to wave up at them with some gusto with the other.

'Strange outfit for sailing,' commented Capstan, who'd never seen a scuba diving sailor before.

'The boat does seem to be half-full of water, sir, so maybe that's why he's wearing the diving gear?'

'Perhaps,' said Capstan, although he didn't think it was likely. 'But what's he doing sailing a dinghy half-full of water in the middle of a planet that seems to be completely devoid of land?'

'Maybe he's taking part in a sailing regatta, sir?'

'What, on Ganymede?'

'Well, they seem to have the right amount of water for it.'

'That's as may be, Dewbush, but if so, then where are all the other boats?'

As the sailor continued to wave at them, but now with even greater enthusiasm, Dewbush said, 'I don't know, sir, but he certainly seems pleased to see us.'

'Anyway, Dewbush, somehow we need to get down there to see if he knows where the baked bean factory is.'

'Yes, sir, but I'm not sure how we're going to be able to do that. Space Police cars can't float, sir. They're only supposed to be used on land and in space, and I'm fairly sure that I read somewhere that if water gets up the exhaust, then the engine will cut out and we won't be able to start it again.'

Capstan thought for a moment before asking, 'Is there some way for me to wind my window down? I could then lean out and try to speak to him from up here.'

'There's a button on your door's armrest, sir. The one marked with the symbol of a window.'

Seeing the button in question, Capstan was just about to depress it when he thought to ask, 'And I can definitely breathe the air outside?'

'The computer says you can, sir, but you may want to be ready to wind it back up again if you find that you can't.'

With that total lack of assurance, before committing to opening up the window fully, Capstan nudged it down an inch, and as a sudden scream of wind whistled past, he shoved his larger than average nose out through the gap and tentatively sniffed at the air outside.

'It seems all right,' he said, a moment later. 'OK, try to bring me as low as you can to the boat, and I'll see if I can have a word with him.'

However, it quickly proved to be virtually impossible for Dewbush to do so, as the boat kept being lifted up and down on the waves and was heaving to and fro as it did. And the manner in which it was doing both was so unpredictable that Dewbush had no idea when the boat was going to come charging straight towards them.

After having done the best that he thought he was able to do, without either hitting the boat's mast or being swallowed by the ocean underneath, he called over to Capstan, 'I think that's about as close as I can get it, sir.'

Hearing that, Capstan wound his window all the way down. With the boy appearing to be doing all that he could to keep clear of the flying car that seemed to have become intent on trying to sink him for no obvious reason, and with the sounds of howling wind and crashing water thundering around his ears, Capstan yelled out, 'Excuse me, but I don't suppose you know if there's a baked bean factory anywhere nearby?'

Judging by the look on the boy's face, what could be seen of it from behind his diver's mask, it didn't seem as if he had any idea what Capstan had just said. Subsequently, Capstan cupped his hands together and shouted, 'DO YOU SPEAK ENGLISH?'

There was still no sign that he understood, so Capstan tried again, but this time deciding to shout even louder and to say the words slightly differently, thinking that the combination of doing both would definitely help.

'ENGLISH SPEAKY, DO YOU?'

But by then it was fairly obvious that the young sailor didn't, as he called back, 'Nire itsasontzia hondoratzen ari da! Ezin al duzu lagundu?!' which neither Capstan nor Dewbush could even remotely understand.

'Sounds like we have a bit of a communication problem, sir,' said Dewbush. 'Why don't you try using Dongle Translate?'

'Dongle Translate?'

'Yes, sir. It's what we always use under such circumstances.'

Taking one hand off the steering wheel, Dewbush pulled out his touch-tech PalmPad, opened up the relevant app and handed it over to Capstan.

'I've set it to Auto-Detect, sir. If you hold it out and get him to talk again, it should tell you what language he's speaking.'

Taking it from him, Capstan leaned out of the car window again and called out, 'Would you mind repeating that for me please?' He then held out the touch-tech device with one hand and used the other to cup around his ear by way of signifying that he was awaiting an answer.

The wetsuit clad boy seemed to understand, and called out, 'Nire itsasontzia hondoratzen ari da! Ezin al duzu lagundu?' which sounded very much like what he'd said the last time.

When he seemed to have finished, Capstan stared down at the screen.

'It says the language is Ganymede.'

'He must be a local then, sir.'

Capstan was about to question his subordinate as to where else he thought the boy might be from, when he heard Dewbush say, 'If you press the green button, sir, it should translate what he said.'

Doing as he was told, a moment later a mechanical voice that seemed devoid of all humanity came back with, 'My boat is sinking. Can you help me?'

'Sounds like it's working, sir. Now try asking him if he knows where the baked bean factory is again using the touch-tech.'

Capstan nodded, and repeated the same question, but this time speaking into the PalmPad. Then he leaned out of the car window, and holding out the device as far as he could towards the boy in the now half-submerged dinghy, pressed the green button.

'Badakizu non labean fabrika bat dago?' came out the same robotic voice.

But still the boy looked confused, so in an effort to help, Capstan sang out the slogan from the TV ad.

'Meanz Baked Beanz?'

'Ahhhh! Meanz Baked Beans!' repeated the boy, nodding his head with a toothy white grin. 'Bai, bai, bai nire itsasontzia hondoratzen ari da. Salbatzen baduzu, erakutsiko dizut!'

Bringing himself back inside the car, Capstan said, 'I think we're making progress, Dewbush. He certainly seemed to have heard of the Meanz Baked Beans TV ad!' and he pressed the green button to hear the translation of what the boy had said.

'Yes, yes, yes, but my boat is sinking. If you rescue me, I will show you.'

'Sounds like he does, sir,' commented Dewbush.

'It also sounds like his boat is sinking, which would explain why it's full of water,' deduced Capstan. 'Tell you what. If you can bring me a little closer, I'll climb into the back and try to pull him into the car from there.'

'I'll do the best I can, sir,' said Dewbush, feeling that he was quite close enough already.

As Capstan wound the window up, he handed back the PalmPad, took his seatbelt off and began clambering over the front seats into the back. There he put that seatbelt on, tested it to make sure that the clasp was secure and that it extended out and locked when pulled hard as it should, and then pushed open the back door.

Once again the wind whistled about him as the little wooden dinghy leapt ever-closer towards him. Leaning out as far as he could, with the seatbelt preventing him from falling into the ocean below, Capstan extended his hand out towards the boy and shouted, 'JUMP!'

Seeing what was happening, the boy stood up, and with one hand keeping a hold of both the tiller extension and the mainsheet, he stretched the other out towards his rescuer. But despite both Capstan and the sailor doing their very best to reach each other, they weren't even close.

'I can't get to him, Dewbush,' said Capstan, between breaths. 'Can't you bring the car any nearer?'

'I'll try, sir, but the boat just won't stay still!'

Just as he said that, a wave lifted the boat up, and as it rocked over towards them it looked as if the red-flippered boy was about to fall overboard. But at the very last moment he leapt up, and just managed to take hold of Capstan's outstretched hand.

Using his other hand to take hold of the boy's wrist, Capstan had to use all his strength to heave the boy up, into the car, until he was safely sprawled over the back seat, gasping for breath, like a fish who'd become bored of swimming under the water and had decided to have a go at hitchhiking instead.

CHAPTER TWENTY

ONCE THE RESCUED scuba diving young sailor had caught his breath and it was clear that he was OK, Capstan closed the rear door and clambered back into his normal position in the front. With the aid of Dongle Translate, the boy then directed them towards his home from where he promised they'd be able to find the baked bean factory they were looking for.

About ten minutes later they could see, over on the horizon, what he'd led them to. It wasn't dry land as such, but more like a giant island constructed of wood and other unidentifiable floating objects. Only as they drew closer did they realise that it wasn't just one single island, but was in fact a collection of hundreds, possibly thousands of different raft-like structures, all grouped together and each with a little flat-roofed wooden cabin sitting on top.

'Hori da nire etxea! Hori da nire etxea!' called out the boy, pointing over Capstan's shoulder.

'What did he say, sir,' asked Dewbush.

With Capstan now using his own PalmPad for translation, he pressed the green button and the touch-tech device said, *That's my home, down there. That's my home, down there.*

'That must be his home, down there,' repeated Capstan, feeling it somehow necessary to say it again.

Their rescued passenger was pointing at one particular raft perched on the edge of the floating island, where a group of three people, all seemingly wearing the exact same scuba diving gear as the boy, had gathered to stare up at the approaching flying object.

'Nire familia!' exclaimed the boy. 'Nire aita dago, eta nire ama. Lurraren hizkuntza hitz egiten dute eta labean fabrika fabrika non dagoen esateko gai izango dira.'

'What did he say that time, sir?' asked Dewbush.

Pressing the green button again, the touch-tech device said, *My family! My father is there, as is my mother. My father speaks the Earth language. He'll be able to tell you where the baked bean factory is.'*

'Looks like it's his family,' said Capstan, translating the translation once again. 'And that his father speaks English and he'll be able to tell us where the baked bean factory is.'

As they grew closer, and noticing that every single person they could see going about their business on the floating island of rafts all seemed to be wearing the exact same wetsuits with the bright red flippers and masks, Dewbush thought to ask his boss, 'Do you think they're *all* divers, sir?'

'It certainly looks that way, Dewbush. Maybe

they're members of the same local snorkelling club.'

'Anyway, sir,' continued Dewbush, 'I still can't see anywhere to land.'

Indeed, although the island of rafts was vast in size, every square inch of it seemed to be serving some sort of necessary domestic purpose.

'How about on top of their cabin?' suggested Capstan.

'Would it take the weight, sir? I'm not sure it looks sturdy enough.'

But Capstan thought it looked as if it would, and turned around to ask what their rescued passenger thought.

'Do you think we'd be able to land on top of your cabin?'

After the wetsuit clad young sailor listened to the translation he smiled at Capstan and with a confident nod, said, 'Aitonak gure etxea eraiki zuen. Etxea oso gogorra da!'

Pressing the green button, the translation came out as, *'My grandfather built our house. It is very strong.'*

'I suggest you land on the roof,' said Capstan. 'If it collapses, we can simply blame the boy's grandfather.'

'Right you are, sir,' and following orders, the lieutenant proceeded to ease the car down as gently as he could.

About a minute or so later, Dewbush had rested it somewhat precariously on top of the structure that was no bigger than your average Earth family double garage, and which creaked and groaned under the weight as if in protest at being used as a makeshift car park without anyone having thought to commission a structural survey before doing so.

After Dewbush reminded him that he'd need to put on his gravity-coat, and once he'd wriggled into it whilst still sitting in the passenger seat, with due caution, Capstan emerged from out of the car and opened the rear door for their rescued passenger.

As soon as it was open, the boy jumped out as if he'd been sitting on an industrial-sized spring, and as he did so a collective gasp rose up from his awaiting family, followed by excited chatter as they all rushed forward to help him down off the roof.

As he began his descent, he called to them, 'Nire txalupa lehortzen hasi zen eta giza gizon horiek salbatu ninduten!' Once he was down safely, they each took it in turns to give him a big hug, followed by a firm shake of the hand.

Dewbush also donned his gravity-coat, and joined his boss to stand beside the car and stare down at this scene of blissful family reunification, both thinking the same thing: that it looked as if, by rescuing this boy and returning him to his family, they'd done something useful, for a change.

Having welcomed his son back into the fold, the tallest of the scuba diving family gazed up at Capstan and Dewbush, and calling up to them, asked, 'You're humans, I take it?'

Capstan thought the time had come to make a formal introduction, and pulling out his space police ID, said, 'We are human, yes! We're actually Space Police. I'm Detective Inspector Capstan and this is my colleague, Lieutenant Dewbush.'

'I just can't say how very grateful we are to you for rescuing my son. I bought him that dinghy for his last birthday, flat-packed from YouGet, but I probably shouldn't have done. I only meant to buy him a fishing rod, but the dinghy was on special offer and our YouGet machine was being particularly persuasive that day.'

'I fully understand,' said Capstan, who did, and was grateful to meet someone else who also struggled to decline YouGet's various enticing offers.

'My name is Mallum,' continued the tallest of them, placing a large black hand over his chest. 'I am Akinda's father, the boy who you so graciously rescued.' He then turned to look down at another wetsuit clad boy, but a slightly smaller version. 'This is my other son, Kai, and beside him my wife, Akimbo. Would you care to join us for tea?'

'You have tea?' asked Capstan, suddenly feeling rather parched.

'And cake. Won't you come down and share it with us?'

153

Neither Capstan nor Dewbush could remember the last time they'd had anything to eat or drink, let alone tea and cake, and not waiting to be asked twice, clambered down from the roof to join this peculiar family of scuba divers whose elder son they'd rescued from what could easily have turned out to be a long and rather boring swim all the way home.

CHAPTER TWENTY ONE

ONCE THEY'D CLIMBED down off the roof, had shaken hands with the boy's family and had been ushered into the double garage-sized cabin that their car was parked on top of, something dawned on Capstan that he probably should have picked up on a long time before that. As they gathered inside, he realised that they weren't wearing navy blue wetsuits, diver's masks and bright red flippers after all. What he'd assumed to be wetsuits was actually their skin, the flippers were their feet, and what he'd thought had been diver's masks were what their faces just happened to look like. And as he let his mind ruminate on that hitherto unknown fact for a while, he and Dewbush were invited to take a seat around a rustic sort of a table that looked as if it was made of sun-bleached driftwood held together with different coloured lengths of fishing line.

Shortly afterwards they were both presented with dark ceramic earthenware cups into which tea was poured by the wife. When they'd established who wanted milk and sugar, and had each been given a large slice of chocolate gateaux, Capstan decided to do his best to ignore the strange physiques these humanoid creatures seemed to have and asked the

155

boy's father, 'May I enquire how you learnt to speak English so well?'

'I studied it at university,' the weird looking man-thing began. 'It was during that time when I went to live in the United Kingdom of America for my year's work placement. But that must have been, what – thirty of your Earth years ago now.'

'And what did you do when you were there?' asked Capstan, continuing to make polite conversation whilst doing his best not to stare directly at his face.

'I worked as a cleaner for Meanz Industries.'

'So you've heard of Meanz Baked Beans then?'

'Of course! I'm now their Health and Safety Manager. And as you can see,' he said, as he stood up from the table to pad over to a cupboard on the wall just to the right of a sink, 'one of the perks of the job is that we get just as many tins as we like!' With that he opened up the cupboard door to reveal dozens of them, all stacked on top of each other.

'Wow!' said Dewbush, sitting beside Capstan, clearly impressed. Since the demise of what used to be called a "supermarket" back in the latter part of the 21st Century, it was rare to see any one product displayed in such numbers like that. However, that did at least explain why Capstan didn't seem to think anything of it. He'd seen tins of baked beans stacked neatly on a shelf loads of times before, and probably just about every time he'd popped down to his local

Safebusy's. But that was before the popular chain store had gone the same way as Blockbusters and Woolworths, about three hundred and fifty years earlier.

But at least the subject of Meanz Baked Beans led neatly into what they'd come all that way to find out; and with that in mind, Capstan asked, 'So you know where the factory is? It's just that we couldn't see it when we arrived and assumed that we'd been given the wrong address.'

'You probably had the right address, but as you may have realised by now, we don't have any land left.'

'But you used to?'

'We did, yes. It was only when we started terraforming and Ganymede heated up much faster than expected that we lost it all. That was when the ice caps melted and we had what became known as the Uholde Handi.'

'The Holdy Handy?' asked Capstan, wondering just exactly how holding hands could have led to the ice caps melting.

'The Uholde Handi was the great flood,' explained Mallum, and let that hang there as a solemn silence fell around the cabin. 'We lost a number of good friends that day,' he continued, moments later. 'Many didn't make it.' Looking around at his family, he added, 'We were amongst the lucky few who managed to survive, and now we live here, on Hiriko Hainbat Gauza

157

Flotatzaile, the City of Many Floating Things.'

'So there's no more land on Ganymede then?' asked Capstan.

'Not that we know of, no.'

As fascinating as all this was, the creature still had not answered Capstan's first question, so he decided to ask it again.

'So, do you know where the Meanz Baked Bean factory is?'

'It's in Mundau.'

'And where's that?'

'Under the ocean. It's where all the Gannars live.'

'The Gannars?' asked Capstan, wondering if it would help if he started using Dongle Translate again.

As Mallum resumed his seat at the head of the table, he started to give them a brief overview of Ganymede's history.

'There are two species of Ganymedians,' he began, 'the Gannars and the Gannets. Gannars all live in Mundau, the city under the ocean, and we live up here, on Hiriko Hainbat Gauza Flotatzaile.'

'And so you're Gannets?' asked Capstan.

'We are,' he replied, with a proud look in his eye.

'And why do they live under the water but you live up here?'

'They built Mundau before we started the terraforming process, before the great flood. They must have suspected what was going to happen when they did, but elected not to tell us.'

'But why wouldn't they have told you something like that?'

'Unfortunately, our two species have never really seen eye to eye. Gannars have always considered themselves to be superior to us. I suppose they're naturally more academically minded, but we Gannets have always been more physically able. We also have different coloured feet. As you can see, ours are a vibrant red colour whilst theirs are more of a wimpy yellow. Anyway, the rumour is that they must have hoped the great flood would wipe us out, but they were wrong.'

After taking a sip from his tea, Mallum asked, 'And what's Space Police's interest in the Meanz Baked Bean factory?'

'It's a line of enquiry we're following,' said Capstan. 'A frozen Fish Finger was stolen from a museum back on Earth, and we believe that whoever makes the baked beans may have had something to do with it.'

'That would be Gorgnome Obadiah. He bought the Meanz brand a few years ago and re-established the factory down in Mundau, using us Gannets as basically a cheap source of labour. But I wouldn't go anywhere near him if I were you. He's the self-elected ruler of Ganymede, and runs the place like some sort of military dictator. I've never met him but those who have say he's a complete psycho nut-job.'

Having met a few psycho nut-jobs in his day, one of whom was his old Chief Inspector, Capstan was undeterred. 'Unfortunately we're going to have to take a look at the factory, whether it's owned by a psycho nut-job or not. I don't suppose it would be possible for you to take us there?'

'I don't see why not, but it's closed today. It's our weekend. I can take you down first thing tomorrow though, and you'd be more than welcome to stay the night here. It's the least we can do for bringing Akinda back to us in one piece.'

CHAPTER TWENTY TWO

CAPSTAN AND DEWBUSH enjoyed the family's hospitality that evening thanks to a rather long game of Intergalactic Uno and a bottle of Surströmming, a vodka-like drink made from fermented fish. Dewbush in particular had a great time playing the Uno game, and afterwards they slept surprisingly well, probably because they'd both drunk too much of the vodka. It hadn't been their intention to get drunk, but Dongle Translate said the phrase "This product must be drunk sensibly" that was written in Ganymede on the label, and in bold capital letters, in English meant "This product will leave you feeling sensible after being drunk", which it hadn't, not by a long way. So having finished the entire thing between themselves, Capstan and Dewbush passed out, arm in arm on the floor, like a couple of male students who'd arrived at a party feeling sober and heterosexual only to find that by the end of it they were surprisingly drunk and completely gay.

The next morning, Dewbush woke himself and Capstan up by shouting, 'INTERGALACTIC UNO!' really loudly in his sleep, before making the embarrassing realisation that they must have slept the entire night effectively together. At least that was what

161

it must have looked like to their hosts, who had draped a gravity blanket over them at some point, probably to help prevent them from floating around the cabin during the night and waking the children.

After breakfast, Mallum took them down to the edge of their island home where a beautiful sixteen-foot highly polished wooden dinghy was moored, and as they watched him climb in to begin hoisting the jib, Capstan asked, 'You go to work in that?'

'Of course,' Mallum replied, as he secured the jib's halyard at the base of the mast and went aft to begin doing the same thing with the mainsail. 'You do both sail, I take it?'

Capstan glanced over at Dewbush. 'Well, I've been in the odd sailing boat in my time. How about you, Dewbush?'

'Unfortunately, I've never been in a boat before in my life!'

'Don't worry,' replied Mallum. 'If you two just sit at the front, you can tack the jib and I'll do the rest.'

Assuming he'd tell them exactly what he'd meant by "tacking the jib", and how they'd be able to do it, as Mallum held the boat steady Capstan tentatively climbed aboard.

'If you could sit on this side here,' he directed Capstan, 'and you over here,' he continued as Dewbush followed his boss on board, 'as long as you don't stand up at any time, especially when we're gybing, you should be fine.'

As Dewbush gazed around at the complex system of control lines, he asked, 'And what would happen if we did happen to stand up when you gybed?'

'Then you'll probably be knocked unconscious by the boom, fall overboard and drown.'

Capstan and Dewbush turned to stare at him.

'Just kidding!' he said, giving them both a wide toothy grin.

Hearing that, Dewbush was about to formally charge the alien creature under Section 57.4 of the Socially Sensible Act 2367 for telling a joke in a public place when Capstan placed a steadying arm on his shoulder, caught his eye and shook his head at him.

Realising his boss was right, and that attempting to arrest someone in a dinghy probably wasn't a great idea, even if it was quite a large one, he remained silent and faced forward again.

In case his lieutenant changed his mind and began the formal arrest proceedings, Capstan thought he'd move the subject along from having been told the one about the man in a dinghy who'd stood up during a gybe, was knocked unconscious, fell overboard and drowned, which to his mind didn't sound like much of a joke at all, and asked, 'So how do we do that "tack the jib" thing you mentioned?'

'Ah, right. That's simple. If we're on the starboard tack, when I call out 'Ready about!' you un-cleat that line there. Once you've done that you say, 'Ready!' Then I'll say, 'Lee ho', and I'll steer the boat around and bring the mainsail over. As soon as we're on the new tack, your colleague needs to pull on that line there and secure it to the other cleat, and we'll be ready for the next tack.'

Judging by the confused look on their faces it was clear that neither Capstan nor Dewbush had a clue what he was going on about, so Mallum said, 'Don't worry, it will be more obvious when we're actually sailing.'

'What's this thing here?' asked Dewbush out of curiosity, as he pointed at an intricate system of pulleys lying between the base of the mast and about a quarter of the way up the boom.

'That's the kicker. One of you will need to pull it in when we're beating to windward and then let it out when we're either reaching or on a run.'

That just left Dewbush even more confused, so he decided to pretend that he'd never asked the question and to let his boss deal with it when the time came.

As the dinghy's bright white sails gently flapped above their heads in the cool breeze, with a cheerful tone Mallum asked, 'Right, are you ready?'

Despite neither Capstan nor Dewbush feeling that they were anywhere close to being ready, they both nodded dutifully; and as Akinda and Kai came down to the edge of their floating home to wave goodbye to their father, as they did every morning that he sailed off to work, in their native tongue Mallum asked, 'Could you cast us off, please, boys?'

Delighted to show off their skills, Akinda untied the bowline and Kai the aft, and after throwing the warps into the boat, Akinda pushed the bow off from the edge of what was effectively a pontoon. Mallum then sheeted in the sail which caught the wind and pushed the whole boat over to port before he sat on the starboard side and hiked out so that his weight flattened the boat out. The three of them then began sailing away from the City of Many Floating Things, turning to wave goodbye to the boys behind them as they did, who were still standing on the pontoon, waving and smiling back.

CHAPTER TWENTY THREE

'ARE WE NEARLY there yet?' asked Dewbush, who was beginning to feel the negative effects of having drunk so much Surströmming the night before. Either that, or he was naturally prone to seasickness, and therefore a life at sea probably wasn't for him, unless it involved lying in a well-sprung bed on board some massive cruise ship that was so big, it wouldn't keel over even if it was set upon by an ovulating blue whale.

'It's just up ahead,' replied Mallum, giving reason for Capstan and Dewbush to do their best to look past the jib sail blocking the view immediately in front of them to see what it was that they were supposedly heading towards.

On the horizon, and in the planet's naturally dim light, they could just about make out what looked to be a massive curved wall that seemed to rise out from the middle of the ocean. At the same time Capstan noticed that they weren't alone. Far from it. There were dozens upon dozens of other sailing craft, all different shapes and sizes, and all seemingly headed for the same destination.

Seeing what he was looking at, Mallum explained, 'It's rush hour. They're all Gannets from Hiriko

Hainbat Gauza Flotatzaile, making their way in to work.'

'And what is that structure, up ahead?' asked Capstan, who was actually quite enjoying himself as he always seemed to whenever he found himself taking a trip in a sailing boat.

'It's Mundau's harbour. It's a fully-enclosed cylindrical wall that's about a mile in circumference and goes all the way down to the ocean floor. It was built before the great flood. We'd no idea what it was when they were building it, but once the waters rose it became fairly obvious that it had been designed as a gateway into the heart of Mundau, and one that would allow an unrestricted flow of traffic in and out of the city, despite the fact that the rest of the planet had been flooded.'

As they sailed ever closer, Capstan began to get a feel for the wall's immense size. He also noticed that spaced equally along the top of the wall were a series of turrets, each with two lifeforms who seemed to be peering down at them, wearing black army-type helmets and looking as if they were carrying guns the size of bazookas.

'And who are they?' he asked, with a note of concern as he pointed up towards the turret closest to them.

'That's Obadiah's private army,' replied Mallum. 'And as you're both neither Gannet nor Gannar, I think it's probable that they'll be asking to see your IDs.'

About ten minutes later, they'd reached a series of floating pontoons that stretched out from the high harbour wall. There, all the crews that had arrived with them were busy securing their boats to the moorings and taking down their sails. Once Mallum had done the same, he led Capstan and Dewbush over to a steel staircase that had been secured against the wall which took them all the way up to the very top, about a hundred feet up in the air.

There they joined one of many queues of Gannets, all lining up to be allowed through some sort of border control. Whilst standing there, Capstan and Dewbush began to attract more attention than they'd have liked. But that probably wasn't surprising, after all, they were the only humans there, and their flat white faces certainly stood out against the dark peculiar-shaped heads of all the Gannets. Subsequently it wasn't long before Obadiah's private army also spotted them, and two of them flip-flopped their way down the line, bazooka-sized guns at the ready, looking like a couple of yellow-footed Nazi ducks who'd just been given the guns for Christmas and were looking for a couple of targets to test them out on.

As they approached, Capstan and Dewbush instinctively reached inside their coats to pull out their

IDs.

'LORTU ESKUAK NON IKUSI DITZAZUN!' shouted the taller of the two private army Gannars, as he pointed his gun in their general direction.

'They're suggesting that you get your hands out where they can see them,' translated Mallum, before taking a half-step away from Capstan, to whom he happened to be nearest, as he knew that Obadiah's private army had a reputation for shooting first before asking questions. Actually, that wasn't true. They had a reputation for shooting first without bothering to ask any questions at all.

With Capstan and Dewbush's hands now held high in the air, and with all the Gannets who'd been in the same queue now backing off to give any flying projectiles every possible chance to miss them, Capstan called out, 'We're from Space Police!' and then looked over at Mallum, hoping he'd feel obliged to translate that for him.

Fortunately for them, he did, calling out, 'Erresuma Batuko Space Polizia ari dira,' whilst doing his absolute best to make it one hundred percent clear that he had nothing to do with them, but was merely acting as their translator.

Once it seemed safe to assume that the two gun-wielding Gannars weren't going to open fire, Mallum indicated to Capstan and Dewbush that they should now show them their IDs.

Ever so carefully they again reached inside their suit jacket pockets to pull out their badges and held them up high in the air for them to see. Once they had, Capstan called out, 'I'm Detective Inspector Capstan and this is my colleague, Lieutenant Dewbush.'

'Zer nahi duzu?' asked the tallest armed Gannar, which Mallum translated as being, 'What do you want?'

'We were wondering if it would be possible for us to have a look around the Meanz Baked Bean factory,' asked Capstan, as politely as he knew how.

After Mallum had translated that for them, the largest one again asked, 'Ba al duzu bermerik?'

'They want to know if you have a search warrant?' said Mallum.

'Well, no,' replied Capstan, 'but we don't need one as we only want to have a quick look at it. We don't need to search the place.'

Although the line may have worked on a factory manager in China, it certainly didn't on a couple of heavily armed Gannars working for Ganymede's private army.

Levelling his gun directly at Capstan's head, and with a rather unnerving smile, the taller of the two armed Gannars said, 'Bilaketa-agindu bat ez baduzu, utzi edo burua itzali.'

Looking around at his translator, Capstan asked, 'What did he say?' although he probably already knew.

'He said, if you don't have a search warrant, then

you can either leave or have your ugly white head blown off.'

'Maybe we should come back another time?' suggested Dewbush, who'd had the idea when he saw the other armed Gannar pointing his bazooka-sized gun at his own head.

Unsurprisingly, Capstan was inclined to agree with him, and said, 'I think you could be right there, Dewbush.'

CHAPTER TWENTY FOUR

WITH MALLUM unable to take them back, as he had to clock-in to work or face a firing squad, it was left to the two armed Gannars to escort Capstan and Dewbush off the premises, which they did by marching them all the way back the way they'd come, down the steel gantry steps and then into one of their patrol boats which they kept moored up outside the harbour wall.

Once on board, it only took them about five minutes to be motored back at full speed to Mallum's floating cabin home, which they were able to find amongst the many hundreds of others seeing as it was the only one with a car parked on its roof.

When they arrived, the armed crew didn't bother to tie up, but simply gave the two Space Policeman a hearty shove off the boat to leave them splayed out on the pontoon to end up looking like a couple of penguins who were trying to catch some sun.

As they picked themselves up, Capstan making sure that his bionic leg hadn't been damaged by the fall, and Dewbush dusting off his suit before retrieving his touch-tech PalmPad to check that its glass screen hadn't been smashed, they saw Akinda and Kai staring at them from the cabin's window, which was hardly surprising. They weren't supposed to come back quite so soon. The boys were probably wondering why they had, and more to the point, why they'd chosen to jump out of the motorboat that had brought them back in quite such a peculiar manner, instead of stepping off it like any normal Gannet would have done.

Moments later, both boys came running out of the cabin, as best they could with their little red webbed feet, and when the smaller of the two called Kai beat his big brother down to the pontoon, he called out, 'Zergatik itzuli zara hain laster? Ez al zaituzte utzi?'

With his PalmPad already in his hand, it didn't take long for Dewbush to translate that as, 'Why are you back so soon? Didn't they let you in?'

Pulling out his own touch-tech device, Capstan replied, 'Unfortunately not.'

'They said we needed a search warrant,' added Dewbush.

'What's a search warrant?' asked Akinda, again after being run through Dongle Translate.

'It's a document that gives us authority to search somewhere, but we didn't need one though, did we, sir? I mean, we only wanted to have a look around the place.'

'Who knows, Dewbush, but frankly I wasn't prepared to stand there and argue with them, not when their guns were bigger than ours.'

'Beraz, zer egingo duzu orain?' asked Akinda.

Capstan's PalmPad translated that as, 'What are you going to do now?'

'To be honest, I'm not sure. Somehow we're going to have to get back there, sneak in and take a look at the baked bean factory, but the place is built like an impregnable castle!'

'What's a pregnant castle?' asked Kai, but only because the Dongle Translate hadn't known the word for impregnable in Ganymede and had automatically substituted the closest word too it.

'It means that it has really high walls and lots of guns,' replied Dewbush.

Looking down at Akinda, the elder of the two boys, and speaking into his touch-tech device, Capstan asked, 'I don't suppose either of you two knows of another way in?'

Akinda glanced over both shoulders before beckoning Capstan to lean forward. He then whispered, 'Esate baterako, sarrera sekretu bat da, inork ez daki zenbat gannets hautagairen bat baizik, eta horietariko bat besterik ez da nire aita gertatu baino lehen esateko, gau batean esateko, gehiegi edaten zuenean?'

'What did he say, sir?' asked Dewbush.

Pressing the green button on his touch-tech, the answer came back as, 'You mean like a secret entrance that nobody knows about apart from a select few of us Gannets, one of which just happens to be my father who told us one night when he'd had too much to drink?'

'Yes, exactly like that!' exclaimed Capstan, back into the translation device, and then eagerly awaited the boy's response.

'Barkatu, baina ez dut ideiarik,' he replied, with a sagacious nod.

'What did he say that time, sir?' asked Dewbush, struggling to contain his excitement at finding out if the boy did know of a secret entrance.

Pressing the green button once more, the translation came back as, 'Sorry, but I've no idea.'

Capstan gave the child a hard stare, but he only grinned straight back at him.

Deciding that it was probably best not to take anything that came out of the mouths of two alien boys seriously, he looked over at his subordinate and asked, 'Any thoughts, Dewbush?'

'Not really, sir; other than sneaking in by disguising ourselves as Gannets.'

'You know, Dewbush, that's really not a bad idea!' exclaimed Capstan.

'So it's a good idea then, is it, sir?' asked Dewbush, a little confused as to exactly what his boss meant by the phrase. After all, it wasn't clear. It could mean that he thought it was a really good idea, or that it was an averagely good idea, or maybe it was almost a good idea but hadn't quite made the grade for being a really good one. It could also mean the complete opposite; that it was the worst idea he'd ever heard in his entire life. The phrase was ambiguous at best, and Dewbush assumed it must have been something people used to say back in the 21st Century.

Seeing the confused look on his face, Capstan said, 'I think that it is a good idea, Dewbush. I think we *could* sneak in by disguising ourselves as Gannets!'

Dewbush smiled. He knew that having good ideas wasn't one of his core strengths. He lacked the imagination necessary to come up with them on a regular basis, which his next question only helped to exemplify.

'But how could we do that, sir? They don't look anything like us.'

However, Capstan thought the transformation from human to Gannet would be a remarkably straightforward one. All he thought they'd need was a couple of black diver's masks, two pairs of red flippers and a couple of navy blue wetsuits. He'd be very surprised if YouGet didn't sell the lot, and all instantly available from the one their host family had in the wall of their cabin, like every other household seemed to have throughout the known universe.

CHAPTER TWENTY FIVE

IT TOOK OVER three hours for Capstan and Dewbush to order the correct scuba diving accessories from their hosts' YouGet hole in the wall shopping facility, during which time they'd had to say a very firm "no" to just about everything that was offered to them, from a DIY swimming pool to the water needed to fill it up. The process had proven to be so psychologically demanding that after they'd had lunch with the family, they elected to take the afternoon off.

For the next couple of hours Dewbush played Intergalactic Uno with the children, whilst Capstan caught up on some sleep. Afterwards, the boys persuaded them to go fishing with them whilst waiting for their father to come back from work, which neither Capstan nor Dewbush minded. By then they realised that if they were going to sneak back into the harbour fortress and find the baked bean factory, they were going to need Mallum's help anyway.

So they spent what was left of the working day learning how to fish, or at least Dewbush did, as they only had three fishing rods and Capstan was happy enough just to watch. And it didn't take long for Dewbush to become a seasoned master, not because he had a natural gift for it or anything, but because as he quickly discovered, all he had to do to look like a pro was to hold a baited line over some water that just happened to be teaming with fish.

By the time he'd caught his twenty-second one, the boys spotted a small sailing boat on the horizon, and, thinking that it must be their father coming home from work, abandoned the fishing, saved all they'd caught for their mother to cook for their dinner, and returned to the pontoon to wave at the approaching vessel.

About ten minutes later, as Mallum brought his dinghy up into the wind alongside the pontoon, the boys reached out to grab the fore and aft lines and used them to tie the boat up.

After the father greeted his children, and asked them how their day had been, he turned to Capstan and Dewbush who'd also been watching his boat sail in. 'I'm sorry about this morning. I guess it's not often we get humans coming here, and they were clearly not too keen to let you have a look around.'

'It's not your fault,' replied Capstan, 'but unfortunately we still need to though, and were wondering if you'd be able to help us one more time?'

As Mallum used one of the halyards to ease the mainsail back down the mast, he asked, 'What did you have in mind?'

'We're going to disguise ourselves as Gannets and

sneak in!' blurted out Dewbush, clearly rather excited by the prospect of being involved in such a clandestine adventure.

'Really?' asked Mallum, with a clear note of surprise.

'That's the plan,' said Capstan, 'and we're hoping you'll be able to help us back to the harbour wall and then, once past the guards, show us where the baked bean factory is.'

'Well, yes, I suppose I can, but how are you proposing to disguise yourselves as Gannets? I'm mean, no offence, but you don't look anything like us!'

'We've bought some items off of YouGet which we think will do the trick.'

'Shall we show him, sir?' asked Dewbush, who was itching to try on all the scuba diving gear they'd bought.

'Yes, Dewbush, I think we probably should.'

About fifteen minutes later, Capstan and Dewbush emerged from one of the rooms at the back of the cabin having made a quite remarkable transformation. When they'd stepped in there, they were two flat-faced humans wearing suits and ties, but after they'd emerged they looked almost exactly like two fully grown Gannets. And all they needed to complete the transformation was some ash from the cabin's fireplace on their hands and faces to hide the whiteness of their human skin. They'd even managed to solve the problem of not being able to wear their gravity-coats by having the foresight to buy a couple of weighted diver's belts, an idea Kai had suggested to them when they'd been buying all the other gear.

'What do you think?' asked Capstan, as they flip-flopped their way around the main cabin room, doing their best to mimic the way Gannets walked.

Once their host family had gotten over the shock of just how much they looked like them, they gave them a round of applause, and after that had died down, Mallum said, 'You look good, but I suggest we sneak in for the night shift. That way, as long as you don't say anything, I really can't see the guards noticing.'

CHAPTER TWENTY SIX

BACK ON EARTH, at the White House in Washington to be more geographically precise, President Dick Müller IV stormed back into his Oval Office after finally having his postponed meeting with the ITU. It was the second time that week that he'd been forced to sit down with them, the first being in London for the Intergalactic Trade Summit when they'd decided to vote against him, and by doing so had banned all fishing on Earth. And it was as a result of that rather ill-advised decision that they'd called the second meeting; but it hadn't gone well, not for Müller at least.

'How dare they tell me how to run my planet!' he growled over at his Chief of Staff, Gavin Sherburt, as he sat back down behind his desk.

Gavin had been in the meeting with him, and now stood before his Commander-in-Chief attempting to catch his breath. The President had left the meeting so quickly that he'd had to break into a jog just to keep up with him.

'I mean,' continued Müller, 'what's the point of being President of Earth if I can't do whatever I want?'

As tactfully as he could, Gavin said, 'I suspect they're simply trying to protect their own economic interests, Mr President.'

'By interfering with how I run my planet and making a complete balls-up of it in the process?'

'Um…' answered Gavin. He was unsure as to how best to answer that one, at least not without it sounding as if he was defending the decision of the ITU, which had been that Earth must sign the proposed trading agreement with Ganymede. If President Müller thought for a moment that he was siding with anyone other than him, it would risk not only his job, but probably his life as well. So he decided to assume that the President's question was rhetorical, and subsequently an answer was neither required, nor expected.

'And why the hell should I start buying over-priced fish from what's-his-face anyway?'

Müller now stared directly at his Chief of Staff, looking very much like he did expect an answer to that one.

But Gavin still wasn't keen, so instead decided he was better off offering up the name of the person he was referring to instead.

'You mean Gorgnome Obadiah, Mr President?'

'I KNOW WHO I MEAN, GAVIN, THANK YOU!'

'Sorry, Mr President,' Gavin replied, cursing himself for having been stupid enough to open his mouth.

'They're seriously expecting me to sign a ten year

contract with that half-man, half-seagull, half-gopher type thing, and fork out over $100 billion in just the first six months?'

'It does sound like a lot, Mr President, but as they did mention, with no more fish left on the planet, and with the riots still taking place throughout every major city, and people demanding that they can eat fish again, it is a little difficult to see what choice you have.'

'To be honest, I can't see what was wrong with my wife's suggestion.'

'I don't think there was anything wrong with her suggestion in particular, Mr President. I just suspect that proposing an invasion of Ganymede only about a week after you'd taken over Titan was a little too much for them, especially when there's no other reason to invade other than they seem to have more fish than us.'

'Well, there wouldn't be much point mounting an invasion if they didn't have more of something than us, would there?'

'Probably not, Mr President. But on the other hand, if they had agreed, there'd be little to stand in the way of them banding together to launch their own invasion, but of Earth, simply to get their hands on our milk supplies.'

'I'd like to see them try!'

Gavin didn't doubt that for a minute. The man would probably use that as an excuse to take over the entire galaxy! And in a bid to dissuade him from contemplating the idea of drumming up an intergalactic invasion force, he said, 'I doubt if doing anything that could be considered as actively encouraging an invasion of Earth by the rest of the galaxy would stand you in particularly good stead with our planet's press, Mr President, especially when so many of them are still running stories suggesting the need for another election.'

'And that reminds me, Gavin. If you could pull up a list of all the journalists who've used that word over the last month and have it sent over for my Secret Service Department to take care of, I'd be very grateful.'

'And which word was that,' enquired Gavin, as he pulled out his touch-tech PalmPad.

'Election.'

Before he forgot, Gavin made a careful note of both the offending word, and that he needed to run a Dongle search to identify the name of any journalist who'd been stupid enough to use it to his list of the people his President wanted to have "taken care of". It's not that he agreed with having people assassinated at the whim of his President, but he'd worked out a long time ago that as long as he was the one in charge of the list, it was less likely that he'd end up on it. He therefore made it a priority to keep the list up-to-date at all times in a bid to avoid anyone else being given the job.

'And what about those who've used the word "election" in a supportive way of your ongoing presidency, Mr President?' he asked, hoping to at least prevent any who were innocent from being targeted.

'I think it's probably best if we simply include them all,' said Müller. 'And after you've done that I'd like you to arrange to have the word "election" banned.'

'You'd like to have the word "election" banned?' repeated Gavin, taken completely by surprise. He'd never normally make it sound as if he was questioning one of his President's decisions – in fact that was probably the first time he had – but in fairness he'd never heard the man make a demand that sounded quite so blatantly dictatorial before.

'Yes, please,' replied Müller, before deciding to justify his decision. 'I've been thinking about it for a while now and I think it's the right thing to do.'

'Of course, Mr President.'

'And once it's been banned, I think we need to make its use a federal offence, one that's punishable by death.'

'Great idea!' said Gavin, unsure what else to say. But one thing was certain. This was the clearest evidence to date that the man was beginning to lose not only his marbles but the bag that, until then at least, he'd been keeping them in. However, it shouldn't have been too surprising that he was beginning to go a bit mad. There was a good reason why the Constitution had historically stated that no American president should be allowed to serve more than two four-year terms, let alone someone who was the president of the entire planet, and Gavin couldn't even remember how many terms of office he'd served since then.

'So anyway,' continued Müller, looking a little more cheerful now that he'd done something to remind both himself and everyone else that he was still the elected President of Earth, even if that election had taken place over a hundred years earlier, 'back to the Ganymede conundrum. All we really need is to find a legal reason to invade. Any ideas, Gavin?'

'Um…' he replied. 'Nothing that springs to mind, Mr President.'

'The only other alternative would be to get some sort of leverage on him. Tell you what, get him on the phone for me and we'll have a bit of a chat.'

With a pretty good idea what his Commander-in-Chief had in mind, Gavin picked up the nearest phone, dialled a number and said, 'I have the President of Earth on the line for Mr Gorgnome Obadiah,' before covering over the mouthpiece and saying, 'I'm being put through now, Mr President.

While he waited, Müller pushed his chair back, stood up and began pacing up and down behind it, as he thought about what he was going to say.

A moment or two later, Gavin held out the phone for him, saying, 'Mr Gorgnome Obadiah on the line for you now, Mr President.'

'Put it on speaker phone, will you please,' said Müller, and after Gavin had pressed the relevant button, called out, 'Mr Obadiah, it's Dick Müller here.'

'President Müller, it's an absolute honour.'

'Oh no, the honour's all mine, Mr Obadiah.'

'That certainly is very kind of you to say so.'

Getting straight down to business, Müller said, 'Now I'm sure you're aware that I've been discussing your proposal with the ITU.'

'Which proposal was that?' asked Obadiah, in an apparent attempt to make out that he had so many proposals floating around that he was struggling to keep track of them all.

'You know, the one that would make us contractually obligated to buy your fish for the next ten years, whilst spending a minimum of $100 billion over the first six months at a price of $5,000 per fish.'

'And I assume you've called to accept?'

'Well, that's what I wanted to talk to you about. I'm sure you can understand that were we to agree to it, it would probably be the biggest deal we've ever made.'

'Apart from the defence contract you signed last month with MDK Industries, you mean?'

Müller shot Gavin a questioning look. He wasn't aware his military contracts with MDK Industries were public knowledge.

But neither, it seemed, was Gavin, who just shrugged back at him.

'Well, er, maybe,' continued Müller. 'So anyway, I'd like to invite you down to the White House for the weekend to discuss the contract in more detail.'

'That's exceptionally kind of you, President Müller, but before you go to any trouble, it may be worth you knowing that I don't drink alcohol. Furthermore, I have very little interest in matters of a carnal nature. And unlike that idiot Lord Von Splotitty, I'm not so stupid as to ever allow myself to be filmed doing something I'd no doubt regret, with a collection of your most bendy young prostitutes who probably don't even know what the word regret means.'

'How the…' Müller was about to ask how the hell he knew about that, but realised that doing so would be an open admission of guilt on his behalf, and for all he knew the creature he was talking to was having the conversation recorded. So instead he said, 'Now listen, Mr Obadiah, the bottom line is that as much as I'd like to fork out $100 billion over the next six months for your fish, I wouldn't!'

'I wasn't aware you had much of a choice, President Müller. After all, there's hardly a single fish left on your entire planet!'

'I can assure you, Mr Obadiah, that if one thing is universally certain, everyone, no matter who they are, has a choice. And surprisingly, that includes me!'

'I see,' said Obadiah. 'And what, may I ask, do you think your choices are?'

'Well, for a start,' began Müller, as he desperately searched the depths of his brain for something intelligent to come back at him with, 'instead of spending that money on buying your fish, I could simply invest it into biological printing, which has the potential to give us all the fish we could possibly need and for virtually zero cost once the technology's been established. With that idea, along with a couple of others I don't care to mention, I'm willing to consider your proposal, but only on the condition that we can renegotiate the price down to $1,000 per fish, and that we only have to sign up for a one year contract.'

'That certainly is an interesting offer, President Müller, but unfortunately it's a long way off from the original. And the last report I read about the current state of biological printing was that it doesn't matter how much money they have, the technology simply isn't there and that it's still at least five years until it could realistically become a reality.'

'Well, that's not the report I read,' Müller lied, 'and unfortunately, that's all I'm prepared to offer.'

'May I remind you, President Müller, that I've already brought the price per fish down from $10,000 to $5,000. Now I am willing to omit the need for you to spend over $100 billion in the first six months, although I'm not sure how you'd be able to survive with any less than that. However, that would only be on the condition that you sign the agreement today for the full ten years.'

'Unfortunately, that's not going to happen, Mr Obadiah.'

'And why's that, may I ask?'

'For three reasons,' began Müller. 'The first is that I don't want to. The second is that I don't like you. And the third is a combination of the first two, meaning that I'm damned if I'm going to agree to anything you ask!'

With that, he slammed the phone down, and turning to Gavin, asked, 'How the hell did he know about my video tape of Lord Von Splotitty, and the arms deal with MDK Industries, *and* the report on biological printing?'

'Unfortunately, Mr President, I really don't know.'

'Well, it's very annoying, Gavin. Very annoying indeed!'

CHAPTER TWENTY SEVEN

ABOUT AN HOUR after Ganymede's sun, which Dewbush thought to be considerably smaller than the Earth one with which he was more familiar, had gone down, and with the planet plunged into a total, all-consuming blackness that made the dark side of the moon seem more like the inside of a fluorescent light bulb, it was time for Capstan and Dewbush to have another go at sneaking back inside the underwater city known as Mundau, with the aid of Mallum, the father of the boy they'd rescued the previous day.

With diver's masks that had already begun to steam up over their blacked-out faces, and still wearing their navy blue wetsuits, using candle-lit lanterns to help show them the path they made their way down to the sailing dinghy, lifting their knees as high as they could with each step so as not to trip over the enormous bright red flippers they had on their feet.

Meanwhile, Akinda and Kai had clamped themselves around their father's legs as they pleaded with him over something. It didn't look as if Mallum was going to agree, whatever it was, but he did look as though he was beginning to find having a boy attached to each leg rather annoying, as after attempting to take

191

a third step he gave up, stared down at them, and with an irritated edge to his voice said, 'Ez! Ezin duzu etorri, eta hori da azken!'

Noticing that neither of the two boys seemed particularly pleased with what he said to them as they let go and stood in front of him looking down at their little webbed feet, Capstan asked, 'What were they saying?'

'They want to come with us,' explained Mallum, 'but it's far too dangerous.'

Dewbush stopped dead in his tracks. 'Did you say it was going to be dangerous?'

'I'm sure he only meant that it may be dangerous for his children,' said Capstan. 'Not us.'

Mallum turned to look at Capstan's and Dewbush's blacked-out diver's mask-covered faces, each lit up by the lamps they were carrying. 'To be honest,' he began, 'I'd have thought the plan would be rather risky for you as well.'

'Which part?' asked Dewbush, as his mask began to steam up even more.

'Well, all of it, really,' answered Mallum. 'First we'll have to sail there in the dark, and even though my eyes are more used to it than your human ones, it's still considered hazardous to sail at night, especially as I only have an old compass to help guide us.'

'That's not a problem,' said Capstan. 'Our touch-tech PalmPads have built-in GPS, so I can't imagine we'll get lost.'

'And then there's the getting inside bit, of course,' added Mallum. 'Although your disguises are very good, I doubt they'll pass a close examination. And if they do find you trying to sneak back in again, but this time dressed up as Gannets, it's unlikely they'll be so kind as to give you a lift home. I'd have thought it more likely that they'll simply throw you straight over the harbour wall, a fall which I doubt you'd survive. However, if they catch you sneaking about inside,' he continued, 'then I'd have thought that they'll either shoot you on the spot before throwing your bodies over the wall, or torture you first, before throwing your bodies over the wall, but either way, I think there's a better than average chance that you'll end up being thrown over the wall, whether you're alive at the time or not.'

'Are you sure this is such a good idea, sir?' asked Dewbush. Now that he'd had a chance to think about it, and that he'd just been given a little more information as to what they could expect from their little clandestine operation, he was beginning to have second thoughts. In fact, he'd already had the second thought and was well into the third one, which was that he really didn't fancy going after all. And to support his new line of reasoning, he said, 'I enjoyed dressing up as a Gannet, and everything, sir, but the part about being captured, tortured, shot, and thrown over the harbour wall doesn't sound all that great, and

I was just thinking that it may be a good idea to try and find another way in.'

'Don't worry, Dewbush,' said Capstan, in a bid to placate his apprehensive lieutenant. 'We're only going to have a quick look around and come straight back. We're not going there to try and blow the place up, or anything. And besides, you're forgetting that we're Space Police. I seriously doubt they'd be stupid enough to do anything to harm us.'

Capstan's words seemed to have the desired effect on his lieutenant, who forced a brave smile at his boss, and said, 'I'm sure you're right, sir.'

However, they had done nothing to alleviate Mallum's concerns. In fact, they had only served to remind him just what a psychopathic lunatic Gorgnome Obadiah was reported to be, and that he had seen Gannets thrown over the harbour wall for no other reason than they'd forgotten their dinner money. So he turned to look down at his two children, still staring at their feet, and in Gannymede said, 'Actually boys, you'd better come. But under no circumstances are you to leave the dinghy when we get there. And if there are any signs of trouble, then I want you to sail back here just as fast as you possibly can and call for help. Do you understand?'

Hearing that, the two boys stood to attention, and with a deadly serious expression on each young face said, 'Aitak ulertzen dugu' – 'We understand, father' –

and about a second later, ran round him, climbed into the boat and began heaving up the sails, presumably before he had a chance to change his mind.

'I take it they're coming then?' asked Capstan.

'I thought they'd be able to help with navigation,' he said. 'They're also fine seamen, and will be able to sail back for help, just in case anything goes wrong.'

'Which of course it won't!' added Capstan, more for Dewbush's benefit than anyone else's. He didn't fancy going without his lieutenant, and so was keen to make sure that he wasn't put off the idea any more than he already had been.

CHAPTER TWENTY EIGHT

W ITH ALL FIVE of them having to squeeze themselves into the dinghy, and with Capstan and Dewbush still trying to get used to moving about wearing the massive red flippers, which they'd found hard enough to do on dry land, let alone inside a sixteen-foot sailing boat, they didn't exactly have a comfortable journey. However, it was at least uneventful, and thanks to the GPS app on Capstan's touch-tech device, they didn't get lost either.

Also, Dewbush wasn't overcome by seasickness as he had been that morning, as by that time he'd made a full recovery from having drunk so much Surströmming the night before.

However, once they'd moored up against the harbour wall with all the other boats that had been sailing in with them, all commuting in to begin the night shift, and after Mallum had reminded his children to remain in the boat, the first challenge awaited the two Space Police officers, but it wasn't one they'd even considered before then: the gantry steps leading up to the top of the harbour wall. Capstan and Dewbush's ascent of them that morning had been tiring, but hardly difficult. However, the prospect of doing the same wearing their new red flippers was something else entirely. If they'd struggled to master the art of walking in a straight line with them on, climbing up a 100-foot galvanised steel staircase was hardly going to be easy.

But with purposeful concentration, and by making sure they held on to the hand rail so that when they tripped up, which they did numerous times, they didn't roll all the way back down, knocking over every Gannet walking up behind them as they did, they eventually made it to the top.

Once there, and after taking a brief moment to enjoy the view, they had the more risky task of sneaking their way through security.

'Do your best to act like everyone else,' Mallum whispered over to them, as they joined one of four long queues of Gannets for the second time that day.

'And how do we do that?' asked Capstan, in a similar hushed tone as he glanced around at the Gannets surrounding him, trying to work out how best to pretend to be them.

'Just keep your heads down and look miserable,' advised Mallum.

That seemed easy enough, especially for Capstan, who'd spent most of his life with his head down looking miserable. So the three of them shuffled forward in the queue, staring at their rather large feet with an appearance of being generally disappointed in the world at large, in very much the same way as all those in the queue with them. It was only when Capstan saw that there was an automatic turnstile ahead where each Gannet had to take it in turns to go through by pressing their thumb against a pad on the right hand side that he asked, 'How are we going to get through that?'

'Don't worry,' whispered Mallum to them both. 'As long as we go through together, it should be fine.'

But it didn't look as if it would be fine from where Capstan was standing, as he could see at least six uniformed Gannars, each carrying a bazooka-sized gun, studying the four queues of Gannets and the turnstiles that they were all making their way through, one at a time.

It wasn't long before his subordinate was beginning to wonder the same thing. And when there were only about five people waiting to go through the turnstile ahead of him he turned to Capstan and whispered, 'Are you really sure this is going to work, sir?'

'Well, it is very dark, Dewbush, and the guards aren't all that close. I'm sure if we do as Mallum says, and try to go through as one, we'll get away with it.

With only two more Gannets ahead of them, it was nearly their turn.

'OK, this is it,' whispered Mallum. 'When I place my thumb on the pad, we all push through at the same time.'

Both Capstan and Dewbush nodded their

understanding, and as the Gannet ahead of them went through, they stepped up to the turnstile and Mallum placed his thumb on the pad. With their heads bent low, and looking as miserable as they possibly could, the three of them pushed through the gate as if they were one.

It worked! And as soon as they were through, they flip-flopped their way forward, lifting their knees as high as they could each time they did so that they didn't trip over their giant-sized feet. And still keeping their heads down, Capstan and Dewbush followed Mallum towards a pair of large steel grey doors that lay just up ahead of them.

CHAPTER TWENTY NINE

ONCE THROUGH the doors, Mallum led them to the nearest of about twelve industrial-sized galvanised steel cage lifts, all of which were in use bringing up Gannets finishing their shifts only to be replaced with the ones arriving to begin theirs.

Whilst waiting for the next one to become available, Mallum noticed that Capstan and Dewbush were still staring down at their feet, deliberately trying to look as miserable as possible, so he leaned in towards them and whispered, 'From here on in, there should be fewer guards, so you should be able to relax a little.'

Taking the opportunity to look up and around him, Capstan asked, 'I assume this will take us to the baked bean factory?'

'It will, but it's about a mile down, and the lifts aren't exactly the fastest in the universe, so it will take us a good ten minutes to make it all the way to the bottom, that's if they don't breakdown first, of course. They're hardly the most reliable. In fact, truth be told, they're probably all a little on the dangerous side.'

'Excuse me, Mr Mallum, sir,' began Dewbush, 'but you didn't mention anything about the lifts being "a little on the dangerous side" when you were telling us about the other things that you thought were "a little on the dangerous side".'

'Well, no, but to be honest, the cables don't snap all that often.'

Capstan and Dewbush turned to stare directly at him.

'And may I ask just exactly when the last cable did "snap"?' enquired Capstan, beginning to hope that there was another way down that didn't involve using the lifts.

'Oh, it must have been at least two weeks ago now, but there were only four workers in it at the time, so it certainly wasn't one of the worst lift accidents we've ever had. I think that award goes to the time when the floor of one of the cages gave way when it was crammed full, and as everyone fell out they managed to take six more with them on the way down, who were in the shaft trying to fix the one next to it. But don't worry, the floor on that one is definitely fixed now!'

'And what about the floor of the one we're waiting for?' asked Capstan.

'Oh, um, number ten, isn't it?' he asked, but more to himself. 'To be honest, I'm not sure. At the moment it's number five that I'm most concerned about, but if you could keep that to yourselves, I'd be most grateful.'

'I'm sorry,' said Capstan, 'but I thought you were the Health and Safety Manager?'

'I am, yes. Why?'

'Well, don't you think you should shut number five down if you think it's unsafe?'

'Oh no! We'd have to close them all if that was the case. Besides, until they break, we don't know what to fix.'

'I don't suppose there are any stairs we could take?' asked Capstan, looking around.

'I think I'd prefer to take the stairs as well,' agreed Dewbush, and joined him in seeing if he could spot a sign that pointed to some. But as his diver's mask had begun to steam up again, he wasn't having much luck seeing anything at all.

'Well, yes, there are, but I don't think it's a sensible option. It would probably take you half the day just to make it all the way down, and with those flippers on you'd be more likely to trip up and fall over the side. They're not very wide, you see, and they don't have a handrail. I'd also have thought that the one mile drop to the bottom wouldn't end well. To be honest, I'd have thought you'd be better off being thrown over the harbour wall. At least then you wouldn't have quite so long to think about what was going to happen when you hit the bottom. Besides, the stairs are only used for extreme emergencies, like if an earthquake cracks the harbour wall and submerges the city under about fifty trillion tonnes of water.'

There was something about the way Mallum spoke

that seemed to make doing absolutely everything hazardous to one's health, but that was probably because he worked as the Health and Safety Manager. However, the earthquake followed by a massive flood scenario was certainly a new possibility, so Capstan asked, 'And is that likely to happen, the earthquake followed by a massive flood, I mean?'

'Well, it hasn't happened yet,' replied Mallum. 'But I wouldn't rule it out.'

As Capstan and Dewbush imagined the scene of fifty trillion tonnes of water pouring through a crack in the harbour wall, so drowning just about everyone and everything who happened to be inside Mundau at the time, Dewbush eventually asked, 'Would it be all right if I stayed here, sir? Then I could keep a lookout for guards and whistle down if I see any.'

Capstan was beginning to wonder if it would be OK if they both stayed there, and to ask Mallum to have a look around for them instead. In fact, now that he thought about it, he wondered why he hadn't considered that idea before. Then they could have stayed at his house playing Intergalactic Uno with his children whilst waiting for him to come back to tell them if he'd seen anything suspicious. But as Capstan couldn't think of what sort of a suspicious item they needed to be looking out for, apart from the Final Fish Finger of course, it was probably best if they had a look around themselves, no matter how potentially hazardous the journey down in the lift may be.

'I think we're probably better off sticking together, Dewbush,' Capstan eventually said. 'For a start, what if someone asked you what you were doing? It's not as if you can speak Ganymede, is it?'

'No, sir, but I could use Dongle Translate!'

'I could be wrong, Dewbush, but I think they may just find that the fact you need a translation device to say what it is that you're doing will make them a tad suspicious.'

'I suppose, sir,' agreed Dewbush, just as the lift arrived.

After Mallum heaved open both sets of scissor-cage doors and let all those finishing their shift out, Capstan, Dewbush, Mallum, and about seven other Gannets all stepped inside to begin their descent.

As it slowly rattled and creaked its way ever downwards towards what was effectively Ganymede's ocean floor, the temperature quickly rose to leave Capstan and Dewbush feeling increasingly uncomfortable under their wetsuits. But more importantly, after only a couple of minutes they'd both completely steamed up, and were subsequently unable to see anything at all through their masks except a thick dense fog. But if they couldn't see anything, they could at least hear something, and it wasn't just the noise of the lift. As they continued their descent, the sound of heavy machinery echoed out beneath them.

And the further down they went, the louder the mechanical sounds became until, by the time the lift had reached the bottom, the noise had become so acute that Capstan thought it sounded like he'd just been emptied out into the back of his local council's refuse truck and was in the process of being crushed to death, together with a week's supply of household rubbish collected from every house along the street he used to live in, and the twenty streets before that.

Once Mallum heaved open the doors again he led them directly out onto a wide elevated gantry platform that overlooked an enormous factory, which Capstan and Dewbush were only able to see by surreptitiously lifting up their diver's masks when they hoped nobody was looking.

Spread out before them was the vast factory floor, every square inch of which seemed to be covered in heavy plant machinery that was overlaid by an intricate pattern of thick steel piping blasting out steam over a massive cylinder which had hundreds, possibly thousands, of individual tins lining the outside, like metallic tiles on a hot tin roof.

Raising his voice loud enough for Capstan and Dewbush to hear him, Mallum said, 'This is where the beans are cooked, each within their own tin.'

'I thought they'd have been baked in an oven,' said Capstan, almost having to shout over the noise.

'It's a common misconception that baked beans are

actually baked,' said Mallum. 'The cooking process would be more accurately described as stewed.'

'So why are they called baked beans then?' asked Capstan, who, having spent most of his childhood eating them, was more than a little disappointed to learn that baked beans weren't baked beans at all, but were in fact stewed beans, which didn't sound nearly as nice.

'I've no idea,' said Mallum.

'And how many do you make a day?' asked Capstan, beginning to feel like he was auditioning for a job as a Blue Peter presenter.

'I don't know about an Earth day, but our target is to produce four million cans per shift.'

'That's sounds like a lot,' said Capstan, but only for want of anything else to say.

'It's enough to meet the current demand. So anyway,' Mallum looked round at Capstan and Dewbush who were both holding their diver's masks just above their eyes so that they could see, 'What do you think you're looking for?'

'Something that would connect this place with the Fish Finger that was stolen from the British Museum,' said Capstan.

'It was the final one, you see,' added Dewbush.

'Right, well. As I said before, I've not seen it, but I suppose it could be around here somewhere,' he said, gesticulating at the vastness of the factory.

206

'It certainly is quite a big area to have a look round,' commented Dewbush.

'I suppose we'd better split up,' suggested Capstan.

'But sir, you said just now that we should stick together!'

'I know, Dewbush, but that was before I realised how big the place is that we have to search.'

'But I didn't think we were going to search the place, sir, given the fact that we don't have a search warrant.'

'Yes, but I thought that as we're here we may as well.'

'And what happens if we do split up and one of us is stopped and asked what we're doing, sir?'

It was a good point, especially as it was the same one Capstan had raised with Dewbush about ten minutes earlier. But then he had an idea, and said, 'It would probably help if we each learnt a phrase we could use in Ganymede, just in case we are stopped. Something to help alleviate suspicion.'

The three of them paused for a moment to think of a suitable phrase, before Dewbush said, 'I know, sir. We can say that we're looking for the toilets!'

'Perfect, Dewbush,' said Capstan, and turning to Mallum, asked, 'How would you say, "I'm looking for the toilet," in Ganymede?'

'That would be *komuneko bila nabil*,' answered Mallum.

'Common echo biller na-balls,' said Capstan, doing his very best to repeat back what he'd heard, exactly as he'd heard it.

'Not quite,' corrected Mallum. 'It's *komuneko bila nabil.*'

'Communal echo billiards n'balls,' said Capstan again, but it still sounded nothing like what it was supposed to have.

'Nearly,' said Mallum, but he was being generous.

'Can I have a go, sir?' asked Dewbush, with his usual youthful enthusiasm.

'Be my guest,' said Capstan, 'but it's not as easy as you might think.'

'Well, my mum says I've always been good at languages,' he said, and after he'd taken a moment to arrange the words in his head, came out with, 'Commando's balls nibbled,' and gave Capstan and Mallum a look of triumphant glee.

Supressing a smirk, Capstan said, 'You're right, Dewbush, you clearly are very good at languages, but now that I've had a chance to think about it, I suggest we'd better stick together after all.'

CHAPTER THIRTY

WITH MALLUM ACTING as their guide, and having decided not to split up, Capstan and Dewbush were given the tour of the Meanz Baked Bean factory whilst keeping their eyes open for clues, preferably in the form of a frozen Fish Finger, or even a trail of breadcrumbs that would lead them straight to it.

However, neither of those was found, and at this late stage in his investigation Capstan was becoming increasingly desperate. Having first flown to Cornwall, then to China, and now all the way to Ganymede, he really needed to find some sort of a clue. But as their tour drew to a close, and the only vaguely interesting thing they'd stumbled over had been the crumbs from a half-eaten Hobnob, which weren't the right sort of crumbs at all, they hadn't been able to find anything to tie the Meanz Baked Bean factory to the theft of the Final Fish Finger, and the Chief Inspector wasn't going to be a happy chappy. In fact, he was more likely to be a seriously pissed off chappy, so much so that Capstan wouldn't be at all surprised if he was thrown back into the cryogenic freezing machine he'd only emerged from about two weeks earlier, but this time with a laminated sign blu-tacked to the wall beside it instructing passing cleaners that under no circumstances were they to use its plug for hoovering.

'What's in there?' Capstan asked Mallum, as they passed what looked to be just another door. They'd walked by a fair few during the tour, but none had been of any great interest as they'd opened into either storage cupboards or putrid-smelling toilets, so he wasn't holding out much hope that this one would be any different, and the only reason he'd bothered to ask was that it had a window in it, which none of the others had.

'That's the Meanz Research and Development Department,' answered Mallum.

'And what do they do?' asked Capstan, giving the inside of it a cursory glance through the window.

'Er, they research and develop stuff,' said Mallum, thinking that should have been obvious. 'I'm told they're currently working on creating a Meanz 58 variety.'

Capstan looked away from the window to stare directly at him.

'You mean, there are still only 57 of them?' he asked, wondering what the Meanz Research and Development Department had been doing all these years if they'd not been able to think of another one since the latter part of the 20th Century. And now that he thought about it, as far as he knew there'd only ever been 57 of them, which meant that either they didn't quite understand what the phrase "research and development" meant, or they'd never worked out quite how to do it.

'Apparently,' said Müller.

Whilst they were discussing the exciting possibility of a brand new Meanz variety being created, Dewbush took the opportunity to peer through the door's window, and after he'd lifted up his diver's mask so that he could see more clearly, moments later exclaimed, 'Sir!' and in such a way to catch the instant attention of his boss.

'What is it, Dewbush?'

'I think I've found it, sir!'

'You think you've found what, Dewbush?'

'The Fish Finger, sir!'

'The Fish Finger?' repeated Capstan.

'Yes, sir!'

'What, you mean, the Fish Finger, Dewbush? The one we've been looking for?'

'The final one, yes sir!'

'Are you sure?'

'I'm fairly sure, sir, yes! It's right there, in the middle of the lab on a table, next to a bottle of tomato ketchup. And around it are about five scientists; one of them is opening a tin of baked beans and all the others are holding knives and forks, sir.'

Unable to hide his excitement at having found what they'd been looking for all this time, Capstan shoved his subordinate out the way, saying, 'Let's have a look,' and raising his own diver's mask disguise, peered through the window once again, but this time to have a more serious look.

'My God!' he exclaimed, moments later. 'I think you're right, Dewbush! It is the Final Fish Finger! And it looks as if they're about to start eating it!'

There was a stunned silence as Capstan and Dewbush reflected on the fact that they'd finally discovered what they'd been looking for, only to see it disappear before their very eyes.

Eventually Dewbush asked, 'What do you think we should do, sir?'

It was a good question. If he were honest with himself, Capstan had never really expected to find it. He'd always assumed that whoever had stolen it must have eaten it by now – after all, that's what he'd have done. And if not eaten, he thought that it would have gone off shortly after having been defrosted, and subsequently been thrown away. But whether he thought it had been eaten or thrown in the bin, he'd never realistically thought they'd ever find it; and certainly not inside a baked bean factory on a planet some 390 million miles away from the one it had been taken from, and which wasn't even a planet, but just a large moon orbiting Jupiter. So now that they had found it, he was a little stuck for an answer as to what they should do.

With his boss still staring at it through the window, presumably still thinking what the next step should be, Dewbush had an idea. As soon as he had it, he knew it was controversial, being that they were Space Policeman. He also knew that it would be a risky endeavour. But despite that, he decided to offer it up anyway.

'I think we should steal it back again, sir!'

Capstan pulled himself away from the window to look at his lieutenant, but surprisingly not in a disapproving manner.

'It would be risky, Dewbush,' he said thoughtfully.

'I know, sir, but it's the Final Fish Finger!'

'It would also probably be illegal, being that we're Space Policemen.'

'But would it, sir? I mean, they stole it from us first, so it's only fair that we should steal it back again. And anyway, if they're about to eat it I don't see that we have any choice, sir.'

It was clearly a moral dilemma. If they didn't try and steal it, it would be eaten and subsequently gone forever, but if they did, then they'd effectively be breaking the law, given that they didn't have a warrant to search the lab and therefore weren't legally allowed to take it.

Still unsure, Capstan thought he'd ask the advice of their tour guide, and turning to Mallum, asked, 'What do you think we should do?'

'Personally, I think it's the most irresponsible and downright dangerous idea I've ever heard in my entire life,' he began, 'and if I were you, I'd leave now and get as far away from this place as possible.'

'Right, that's it then,' said Capstan, and staring over at Dewbush, said, 'We're going to steal it back!'

Dewbush grinned at him, but Mallum didn't seem even remotely amused.

'Didn't you hear what I just said?'

'Of course,' replied Capstan, 'but you have to understand that this is the Final Fish Finger we're talking about. If we simply walk away now, without at least trying to take it back, then there's every chance that it will never be seen again.'

Capstan's passionate little speech must have had some sort of effect on Mallum, as instead of saying that they were completely mad and walking away to leave them to it, he said, 'I admire your courage, but I can't see how you'll be able to get away with it.'

'I think we just need to think of some way to distract the attention of those inside the lab, sir,' said Dewbush. 'Then, when they aren't looking, we can simply sneak inside, grab the Fish Finger, and make our way out the same way we came in.'

The plan sounded simple enough; the only question was how they'd be able to distract those inside the lab for long enough for them to sneak in and grab it.

Mallum let out an audible sigh, before saying with

obvious reluctance, 'I suppose I could distract them for you.'

'Are you sure?' asked Capstan.

'It wouldn't exactly be difficult,' continued Mallum. 'All I'd need to do is to go in and tell them that there'd been an earth tremor, and I can't see them hanging around to find out if there was going to be another one.'

'Right!' said Capstan. 'This is the plan. Mallum, you go in and tell them that there's been an earthquake, and that they're all about to die in some sort of massive flood, and when they come out, we run in, grab the Fish Finger and get the hell out of here. How does that sound?'

'Like total and utter lunacy,' said Mallum.

'I thought it sounded rather good,' said Dewbush, with renewed admiration for his still relatively new boss.

With another heavy sigh, Mallum placed his hand on the laboratory's door handle and said, 'Right then, are you ready?'

Capstan and Dewbush looked at each other before answering in unison, 'Ready!'

'Off we go then,' said Mallum. He then knocked on the door, poked his head inside and in Ganymede said, 'Excuse me. Sorry to bother you. It's Mallum here from the Health and Safety Department. We've just detected a minor earth tremor, so we're advising everyone to evacuate the city in a safe and orderly fashion.'

He then stood away from the doorway, clearly expecting what did happen to happen, that the five lab workers immediately stopped what they were doing and began clambering over each other in a desperate bid to be the first out.

When the last of them had run past them, Capstan poked his head in, and, once happy that the coast was clear, snuck inside, gesturing Dewbush to follow.

CHAPTER THIRTY ONE

INSIDE THE LAB, Capstan and Dewbush gathered around the Fish Finger with every intention of stealing it so that they could return it to Earth where they felt it belonged. However, as they stared down at it they found themselves becoming captivated by its crispy golden splendour. After all, this was it, the final one, the last to have ever been made which dated back well over a hundred years and which, until a couple of days before, had been the key exhibit at the British Museum. Since then it had been nabbed during an armed raid, flown 390 million miles to Ganymede, the largest of Jupiter's moons, and had just been saved the fate of being eaten by a group of alien scientists who, judging by the amount of lab equipment that surrounded it, must have already spent a considerable amount of time probing it for some unknown purpose of their own.

They were woken out of their trance-like state by Mallum, who'd found himself guarding the door, and seeing them doing nothing more than standing there, cleared his throat rather loudly. He knew they wouldn't have long before the scientists whom he'd just told that there'd been an earthquake, and that the entire city was being evacuated because of it, began to question the validity of that information, especially as it should be fairly obvious that nobody else was heading for the emergency staircase, all clambering over the person in front of them, screaming as they did so. And as soon as they worked out that they'd been duped, they'd no doubt be sounding the alarm, or at least come running back to see if anyone had eaten their Fish Finger before they'd had a chance to.

'How do you think we should take it back with us, sir?' asked Dewbush, as he began to think of the practicalities of stealing a Fish Finger and then transporting it all the way back to Earth to be reinstated as the key exhibit at the British Museum, without the possibility of it biodegrading in the process.

'I'm not sure, Dewbush,' said Capstan. 'Is there some sort of an air-tight container we could keep it in?'

'You mean like a lunchbox, sir?' asked Dewbush.

'I was thinking more of a Tupperware container, one with a lid.'

But neither of them could see anything like that.

'How about we just put it in a bag, sir?' suggested Dewbush.

'It wouldn't be a bad idea, but I can't see one of those either.'

As they pondered the problem, Dewbush said, 'We probably should have brought something with us, sir.'

'Well yes, of course!' said Capstan, resenting being told the obvious. 'But we hadn't exactly expected to find it lying on a plate about to be eaten by a bunch of aliens, giving us no option but to take it, had we?'

'I suppose not, sir.'

They both thought for a moment before Dewbush suggested, 'What about putting it inside a test tube? There's a rack of them over there, beside that Bunsen Burner.'

From his position by the door, sounding a little stressed, Mallum called out, 'Are you taking it, or not?'

Ignoring him, Capstan said, 'The test tube will have to do. I'll go and grab one, and you get ready to put it inside.'

'Yes, sir.'

'But be careful, Dewbush. If they were about to eat it, it can't be frozen anymore, and that will mean that it's going to be incredibly fragile.'

'I'll do the best I can, sir.'

As quickly as his flippers would allow, Capstan flip-flopped his way over to the other side of the lab, where, nestled inside a wooden rack, were a number of different-sized test tubes. But he couldn't decide which one would be the right size, so eventually he just grabbed the two he thought most likely to accommodate the Fish Finger without either squashing it or allowing it to move around too much. Then, as fast as he possibly could, he flip-flopped his way back to where Dewbush was hovering over the Fish Finger, looking like a wizard attempting to miraculously turn a dissected frog back into an un-dissected one. But what he was actually doing was trying to work out how best to pick it up without it falling apart in his hands as he did so.

He was just about to lift one end up with the index finger of his right hand when Capstan called out, 'Hold on, Dewbush, there's a spatula over there. Let me grab it, and you can have a go with that.'

Without waiting for a response, he flip-flopped his way around to the other side of the table where there was indeed a spatula, possibly the same one used to put it on the plate when the aliens had first started to experiment on it.

Racing back round, or as racing as he could manage, he handed it to Dewbush.

Taking the proffered kitchen utensil, and with Capstan now holding out his two test tubes, Dewbush asked, 'Which one should I put it in to, sir?

'Try the one on the right first.'

'Your right, or my right, sir?'

'Oh, sorry, Dewbush. The one on my right; your left,' and he wiggled the one he meant. 'But if it doesn't look as if it's going to fit without getting squashed down the bottom, then try the other one,' and to make sure Dewbush knew which one he'd meant that time, he added, 'This one!' and gave it a wiggle as well.

'OK,' said Dewbush. 'Are you ready, sir?'

'All set.'

With that, ever so carefully Dewbush slid the spatula under the Fish Finger and lifted the whole thing off the plate, but the very moment he had, the sound of an alarm went off!

'Damn it!' exclaimed Capstan. 'The plate must have been pressure-sensored.'

'WE NEED TO LEAVE, *NOW!*' bellowed Mallum, over by the door.

Knowing they probably had barely moments before they were caught red-handed, or more accurately Fish-Fingered, Dewbush slid their prize down into the test tube Capstan was holding, dropped the spatula onto the table, and flip-flopped his way out.

With the Fish Finger safely deposited inside the test tube in his right hand, Capstan left the other tube on the table beside the spatula and followed after his lieutenant.

When they reached the door, Mallum looked around at them and said, 'When you get out into the corridor, whatever you do, don't run!'

'That's fine by me,' said Capstan. 'I doubt we'd be able to anyway, not with these flippers on.'

'OK, so just walk casually over to the lift shafts and wait patiently for the next one that comes available. As long as we don't look as if we're in a hurry, we should be all right.'

With one final check to make sure the coast was clear, Mallum led them out. Fortunately the lifts were only about fifty yards away, as Capstan and Dewbush found it even harder to walk in a casual manner wearing their giant-sized red flippers than they'd done to walk normally.

Mallum pressed the button to call for the lift, and they waited patiently for it to arrive, doing their best to keep looking down at their feet and not searching the factory for any signs of an armed security Gannar who may have been headed their way.

Inside the lift, Mallum closed the scissor doors and pressed the button for the exit level, and with nobody inside with them, Capstan and Dewbush allowed themselves to breathe a sigh of relief and took their diver's masks off as they'd completely misted up in all the excitement. And as they stood there with the lift slowly ascending, they used their blackened fingers to rub the inside lenses in a bid to clear them so that they'd be able to see.

'We should be all right now,' said Mallum, as the lift rattled, creaked and groaned its way to the very top of the shaft. 'They're generally less worried about people leaving than those coming in.'

But Capstan wasn't at all convinced. That may have been the case at the end of a working day, but he didn't think it would be quite so straight forward with

222

the sound of an alarm still wailing out all around them. 'But won't they be searching everyone trying to leave because the alarm's gone off?'

'I doubt it,' he said. 'We've only got one alarm to cover all emergency situations, so it will take them a while to figure out that this is for something other than a fire or a seawater breach. To be honest, I've never known anything to have been stolen before, so that should be the last thing they'd be expecting.'

Although still not convinced, when Capstan saw the group of scientists from the lab climbing the emergency stairs on the wall over to their left, who must have been spurred on when they'd heard the alarm go off, he felt a little more comforted, especially when he noticed that dozens of factory workers were collecting themselves at the base of the stairs, all clambering over each other and seemingly desperate to escape whatever horrific fate they thought the alarm was giving them advanced notice of.

However, he soon changed his mind as the lift began to creep towards the upper most level where he could see two armed Gannar guards standing beside the doors.

'I hope they're not waiting for us!' said Capstan, as he and Dewbush secured their diver's mask disguises back into position over their blacked-out faces.

'I'm sure they're not,' said Mallum, although without much conviction. 'But just in case,' he continued, 'when we get there, let me do the talking and whatever you do, don't say anything. Is that clear?'

With rapidly accelerating heart rates and their masks having already steamed up again, Capstan and Dewbush nodded their understanding, just as the lift drew level with the top floor. And as Mallum began rattling open the two sets of scissor doors, they adopted the formerly recommended pose of ambivalent depression, by staring down again at their flippers.

However, although their disguises may have been enough for the odd casual glance in a dimly lit factory, they were nowhere near good enough to pass the scrutiny of the guards who'd been told by radio that the Final Fish Finger had been stolen from the lab and that they were to stop and search anyone who looked even vaguely suspicious, which unfortunately for them, they did, especially as one of them was carrying a test tube with what looked remarkably like the stolen item in question propped up inside it.

CHAPTER THIRTY TWO

THE TEST TUBE with the Final Fish Finger was taken from him, and Capstan was led at gunpoint, along with Dewbush and Mallum, past the factory lifts and through a door in the far wall, one which had a sign of a red flipper enclosed within a circle with a solid black line through it.

As they drew closer, Mallum pointed at the sign and whispered over to Capstan, 'That means no Gannets. I've never been allowed inside before.'

Overhearing him talk, the nearest guard shouted, 'ISILDU!' and backed up whatever he'd said by jamming the butt of his gun hard into Mallum's arm.

'Ow!' said Mallum, rubbing the injured limb. And to make sure Capstan was kept in the loop, translated quietly over to him, 'The guard just told me to be quiet.'

With an even harder prod, and straight into the hand rubbing his arm, the guard shouted, 'ITZALAK ESAN DIZUT!'

Making sure he didn't say "Ow" that time, even though it really hurt, Mallum whispered, 'The guard told me to be quiet, again,' clearly determined to make sure Capstan was being kept up to date with what was going on every step of the way.

Hearing that he'd dared speak again, the guard stopped where he was and with one hand, grabbed Mallum around the throat, saying, 'Berriz hitz egiten baduzu, zure ergelak gorringoak moztuko ditut eta arraina jaten eman. Ulertzen duzu?'

As soon as he let go, and they continued on with their journey, Mallum was about to translate that he'd been told that if he spoke once more, the guard would cut his stupid red-webbed feet off and shove them so far down his throat that they'd come out his bum. However, when he opened his mouth to offer that translation, he found that he was unable to talk, which shouldn't have been too surprising as he was struggling just to breathe in and out. So instead of continuing to offer his translation services, instead he quietly pondered whether or not it would be possible for his feet to fit down his neck and then be pushed all the way down until they came out the other end.

With Mallum physically unable to speak, they continued in silence, through the door and into a corridor beyond that was in marked contrast to the factory they'd just been having a look around. The most obvious difference was that it was clean, and when they arrived at what appeared to be another set of lifts, Capstan couldn't help but notice that they were fully enclosed and weren't badly painted steel cages. The doors themselves seemed to be made of highly polished stainless steel and wouldn't have looked out of place inside a luxury five star hotel.

With the single press of a button, the doors pinged open and Capstan, Dewbush and Mallum were unceremoniously shoved inside, followed by the two guards.

Moments later the doors closed and the lift began a smooth, quiet descent. But inside the lift, what had become an awkward silence seemed to be growing louder. The guards didn't say anything because they had nothing to say, and although Mallum was breathing more normally by that time, he was still undecided if his feet *would* fit down his throat, but had at least come to the conclusion that it wasn't worth talking, just in case they had a go and it turned out that they did. And Capstan and Dewbush didn't want to say anything either, as although they too had lots of things that they'd have like to say, like, for example, 'I don't suppose you could let us go?' they didn't see the point, as it seemed unlikely the guards spoke English, and if Mallum translated what they said, there was no telling what they'd do to him.

When the lift reached the bottom, the doors pinged open and they were led out into what appeared to be an underground cavern that had been converted into a luxury apartment at considerable expense. Dominating the elegant well-lit room was a long rectangular dining table draped with an immaculate white cloth, surrounded by twelve high metallic chairs that had been placed evenly around it, looking as if they were there to prevent the table from doing anything silly, like leaving.

To the right of the dining table was a white leather suite consisting of two long angular sofas with a glass coffee table in the middle, all of which faced a fire place where flames crackled with glowing invitation. Over on the far left- hand side of the room was a wall lined with three rows of TV monitors, each alternating between different views of Mundau and its high harbour walls, from the boats lining the exterior base of the wall to the entry point turnstiles, and all the way down to the factory floor. From some of the images on display, it looked as if there were even cameras inside the toilets.

Beneath the bank of TV monitors, leaning back in a black executive's chair, with a pair of bright yellow webbed feet resting on the top of an opaque glass desk, was a Gannar who seemed completely absorbed by the various TV images on display.

Realising that they hadn't been heard coming in, one of the guards coughed loudly, causing the lifeform with his feet on the desk to lift them off, swing them around and stand up.

Seeing that the guards had brought him two humans dressed up as Gannets, and a Gannet who didn't seem to be dressed up as anything at all, with a wide toothy grin he called out, 'You're here, at last!'

and flip-flopped his way over to them, adding, 'Welcome to my underwater retreat.'

As he approached, the guard who now held the test tube with the Final Fish Finger inside stepped forward, held it out and said, 'Horietako bat aurkitu genuen, zure Eminence.'

Taking it from him, the Gannar who appeared to be their host for the day held it up to the light to examine it. And as he gazed up at it he said, almost absently, 'Joan zaitezke.'

The words must have meant that the two guards could leave, as they first stood to attention and then pivoted around and marched straight back into the lift, where they disappeared behind the highly polished doors a few moments later.

With the guards gone, and with the Gannar standing in front of them still gazing up at the golden Fish Finger, Capstan said, 'Excuse me, sorry, but who did you say you were again?'

'Forgive me,' he answered, glancing briefly over at his three guests. He then held the test tube out with the Fish Finger inside it for them to see and added, 'but she's beautiful, don't you think?'

With an ambivalent shrug, Capstan said, 'I suppose.'

'But where are my manners?' continued the Gannar. 'My name is Obadiah. Gorgnome Obadiah, but my friends call me...' but he stopped mid-sentence

229

and stared up at the ceiling that looked as if it had been carved out of solid granite. 'Actually, I'm not sure I have any friends. But anyway, who needs friends when you've got your own planet!' and he looked directly at Capstan and gave him a cold thin smile.

'No doubt you're finding this all highly amusing,' said Capstan, 'but I'd better warn you that we're—'

'Space Police?' interrupted Obadiah. 'Yes, I know, thank you. You're Detective Inspector Capstan and that thing there is Lieutenant Dewbush.'

Dewbush turned around to see if it was another Lieutenant Dewbush he'd so rudely referred to, but when he realised that there wasn't, and that he'd meant him, he turned back and gave Obadiah a very hard stare.

'I've been watching you, you see,' continued Obadiah, and gesticulated to the wall lined with TV monitors. 'Call me a paranoid control freak, but I like to know what's going on around my planet, especially inside Mundau.'

As he guided them over to have a closer look at the monitors, he said, 'I happened to see you when you first tried to get in, although you weren't exactly difficult to miss. It's not often we have human visitors here, and your flat white faces stood out a mile. Actually, probably more like two miles! That's why I instructed my guards to escort you off the premises, back to that squalid festering floating pile of crap your traitorous friend Mallum here thinks of as his home.'

With that he presented the same thin smile to Mallum, who couldn't help but shudder as if he'd just had a bucket of Ganymede seawater poured down his neck.

'But then you made the mistake of dressing up as Gannets and returning to try again. And I thought your disguises were so very amusing,' he continued, giving Capstan's wetsuit a poke with his long bony black finger, 'that I allowed you inside, giving my guards strict instructions to leave you alone so I could amuse myself by watching you. It was only when you eventually managed to find your precious Final Fish Finger, and were then foolish enough to try and steal it, that I raised the alarm and asked them to detain you. So you see, your efforts to find and return it to the British Museum, from where I arranged to have it stolen, have been futile.'

'So, you've been spying on us then?' questioned Capstan, as if it was a criminal offense.

'Of course I've been spying on you! Here, let me show you,' and he led them over to the desk which had a touch-tech display on its surface. 'Now, where was it...' and as he pressed on a re-wind symbol, they looked up at the screens as all the Gannars and Gannets that had been filmed during the course of the day began flip-flopping backwards at twenty times normal speed.

'You can see the date and time on each monitor, so I can go back to exactly the moment I first saw you, which was...here!' and he stopped the footage of all the monitors, and pointed at the one in the very middle. 'There you are! You can see how much your flat white faces show up.'

It was true, they did stand out somewhat against all the hundreds of dark black faces of the Gannets.

'So as I said, I have been spying on you, yes! But what did you expect me to do? Ignore you and let you walk off with what is now my Fish Finger?'

'It's not *your* Fish Finger,' blurted out Dewbush. 'It belongs to the British Museum!'

'Ah, Lieutenant Dewbush, so you can talk after all. I was beginning to wonder. Unfortunately, my surveillance system isn't wired for sound, so I couldn't be sure. However, I'm going to have all the cameras upgraded to have built-in microphones, so next time I'm spying on two Space Policemen wandering around my factory, I'll be able to know what they're saying. But that's my next little project, and it will have to wait. The one I'm currently working on is far more important.'

'And what is that, may I ask?' enquired Capstan.

'Aaaahhhh, I'm so pleased you have! Too be honest, I've been dying to tell someone. Tell you what, why don't I give you the tour.'

'I don't suppose there's any chance that we don't

have the tour?' asked Dewbush. 'It's just that we've had what's felt like one tour already today, and these flippers are making my feet hurt.'

'Tough!' stated Obadiah, and as he turned to lead them along the wall towards what looked like a bookcase, he said, 'Besides, you won't be walking around for very much longer,'

Capstan really didn't like the way he said "walking around" as if it had inverted commas around it, and therefore that it could infer an alternative meaning, and not the obvious one that after the tour they'd be able to sit down and put their feet up.

However, that was what Dewbush must have assumed he'd meant, as he began following him with only the slightest shrug of his shoulders. Watching him flip-flop away, Capstan thought he'd better go as well, closely followed by Mallum, who seemed even more reluctant to do so than Capstan did.

CHAPTER THIRTY THREE

ARRIVING AT THE bookcase, Obadiah turned to wait for everyone else to catch up. Once they had, he smiled around at them before reaching up for one particular book, which Capstan noticed was the old American classic, Moby-Dick. He then pulled down its top corner as if to take it out, and in doing so he must have triggered some kind of an electric motor, as the entire bookcase began rolling away to reveal a small secret entrance that seemed to have nothing but all consuming darkness beyond.

'This is what I like to call my garage,' he said, and stooping over so that he wouldn't bang his head on the top of the doorway, led his three guests inside.

Once they were all through, and were now standing in a cold and near total blackness, he clapped his hands together, the sound of which must have signalled the lights to come on, as a hard electrical snap echoed out all around them and darkness turned to light.

It took a moment for Capstan to comprehend what he saw in front of him. In place of the former darkness appeared a vast subterranean lagoon, and they were standing on what was effectively a pontoon, at the far end of which was what looked like an enormous airship, similar in both size and shape to the ill-fated

Hindenburg. But instead of hovering above the surface of the ground, it was half-submerged under water.

'This is what I call a vacuum trawler,' announced Obadiah, his voice echoing around the underground cavern.

'And what's one of those?' asked Capstan, as he gazed up at the giant-sized object.

Obadiah thought for a moment before answering, 'I suppose a vacuum trawler is a bit like a vacuum cleaner, only bigger.'

'No kidding,' said Capstan.

'And instead of sucking up household dust as it's pushed up and down over a carpet,' continued Obadiah, 'when not docked here it flies around Earth, sucking up millions of tonnes of your stupid planet's cod, and anything else it happens to find along the way, like the odd fishing trawler, for example.'

'So you're the one responsible for the missing fishing trawlers!' declared Dewbush, pleased that they'd at least managed to solve that one particular mystery.

'A brilliant deduction, Lieutenant Dewbush. Well done!'

'And all the fish as well, I assume,' added Capstan.

'My word, you can both do it. Remarkable!'

Deciding to ignore his sarcastic comments, both of which were in clear violation of the Socially Sensible Act 2367, Capstan asked, 'But why go to all the trouble, just for a large number of fish?'

'Well, unfortunately for you and your planet, I don't like humans. Actually that's not true. I *really* don't like humans! You see, I had the misfortune to be brought up on Earth. My family moved there when my father was given the job of Intergalactic Stock Broker for the Instathon Bank, which back then was a rare honour, but that meant that I had to go to an Earth school. At the time I was the only Gannar there, which meant that if people weren't staring at me sniggering, they were calling me names like Flipper Face, Whale Man or Dildo Boy. Even the teachers disliked me. So I sought solitude in my studies, and ended up leaving school with an offer to read Biological Science at Oxford University.

'Once there I thought things would change, but they only got worse. On top of all the name calling, I had to endure physical torture as well, the worst of which was when I was tied up and locked inside an old grandfather clock, leaving me with a permanent fear of cuckoos. And if it hadn't had to be wound up every three days, I'd probably still be there!

'Then I did a Master's Degree in Economics before deciding to follow in my father's footsteps by taking a job with the Instathon, but instead of becoming a stock broker, I went into the higher risk area of intergalactic hedge fund management. Fortunately, I turned out to be exceptionally good at it. Banking is one of those rare occupations where they really don't care what you look like, as long as you can make money, and make money I did.

'Five years later I'd made enough to start working on what had become my obsession, and something I'd been planning ever since my first year at Oxford.'

'And what was that?' asked Capstan, thinking that if the Gannar knew that he was going to give them a rendition of his entire life story, he could've at least offered them a seat first.

'Well, initially my plan was to take over the world; Earth obviously, not this one. But the longer I stayed there, the more I despised the place and every human who'd ever been born on it. So, instead of taking it over, I decided to devise a scheme to see it deprived of its natural food resources, enabling me to one day sit back and watch it become a stark barren landscape, and roll around on the floor laughing as the human species fought over the last scraps of food before turning on themselves, like the zombies featured in so many of your totally unbelievable and always so predictable Hollywood films.

'So, as I said, rather than simply taking over Earth, I decided to move back to my home planet, Ganymede, and take that over instead, which wasn't difficult. Actually, that's not true either, it was quite difficult. First I had to find a way to persuade the intellectually inferior Gannets to hand the planet over to me.

Unfortunately, unlike my own species, none of them seemed to be interested in accepting bribes, and threats of physical violence didn't seem to work either. So instead I decided to just wipe them out by taking a page out of the Bible. Actually it was more like three chapters, the ones about Noah and the Ark, from the book of Genesis. I sold them all the idea of terraforming the planet so that it could become a lush green Garden of Eden, where Gannars and Gannets could live alongside each other in peaceful harmony, just like in that old Earth song.'

'You mean, Ebony and Ivory?' asked Capstan.

Out of idle curiosity, Dewbush asked, 'What was that?'

'It was a pop song back in the 1990s,' replied Capstan, relieved to be able to take a break from having to listen to some psycho alien nut-job's seemingly endless story about how he took over the world in order that he could take over another one, or whatever it was that he'd been going on about for what felt like about two hours.

'It was actually a song from the 1980s,' corrected Obadiah. 'It was a collaborative effort between two popular artists of their day; Paul McCartney and Stevie Wonder. It went to Number One in both what was then called the United Kingdom and the United States of America. The song centred around the racial struggle between black people and white people, back in the day when Earth had black and white people, of course.'

'Black and white people?' asked Dewbush. He'd no idea that the human species used to look like pandas.

'Never mind, Dewbush,' said Capstan, in a dismissive tone. 'It's hardly relevant.'

Obadiah narrowed his eyes at Capstan, before asking, 'And how is it that you know so much about that era from Earth's distant past, Detective Inspector? Are you some sort of amateur historian?'

Answering for him, Dewbush said, 'He's from the 21st Century. He served as a policeman back then and was awarded an ODE along with a King's medal for owning a brewery.'

'It was actually an OBE and two Queen's Police Medals for bravery,' corrected Capstan.

'But he was injured in the line of duty when he was shot in the leg,' continued Dewbush. 'Then they had him cryogenically frozen and he was only defrosted last week.'

'Ah, I see!' said Obadiah. 'Much like your precious Fish Finger!' He smiled around at them all, clearly amused by his own analogy.

'Apart from the fact that I was a Detective Inspector working for the British Police, I'd have to say yes, I'm almost exactly like a Fish Finger,' said Capstan, just about as sarcastically as he thought was possible.

'Anyway,' continued Obadiah, 'I have the song as part of my vinyl collection,' and looking at Capstan, asked, 'Maybe you'd like to listen to it some time?'

'That would be nice, thank you,' said Capstan. He didn't want to listen to it, or any song from the 1980s, but he thought by doing so he could at least delay what he was beginning to feel was the inevitable. Judging by the way this deranged lunatic was telling them absolutely everything about his plans for destroying the human species, he'd clearly no intention of letting them go, and had probably already decided to either lock them up in some dark subterranean dungeon with nothing more than a husk of bread to share between them, or to simply shoot them in the head and throw their bodies over the harbour wall to help feed some of the many billions of fish he'd sucked out of Earth's oceans without having sought permission beforehand.

'Anyway, where was I?' asked Obadiah, who by then had completely lost his train of thought.

Ever helpful, Dewbush said, 'You were telling us the story of two people, one called Ebony and the other Ivory, who were black and white and looked like pandas, and together they wrote a song whilst doing a number one in the toilet.'

Obadiah narrowed his eyes at him, but couldn't tell if he was being deliberately facetious or was just naturally dim. But either way, it had reminded him of what he was saying, so he continued.

'Of course I knew that terraforming Ganymede would heat the planet up enough to melt the ice caps and flood the place, so at the same time I had Mundau built, along with my little underwater retreat. And whilst waiting for the planet to warm up, I designed my vacuum trawler, in preparation for the next stage of my plan.'

'The one where you flew around Earth, sucking up all the fish?' asked Capstan.

'That's right, that one! But the best part is that I'm now on the verge of signing an agreement with that moronic President of yours, after which I'll be able to sell the very same fish I've stolen, straight back to Earth, and at five times what they currently pay!'

However, by then Capstan had found rather a large hole in his plan.

'But you're hardly going to be able to starve Earth if you sell all the fish straight back to them, are you?'

'Yes, well, for now I need to recoup my losses.'

'And another thing,' Capstan continued, 'Ganymede isn't a planet. It's just a moon that orbits Jupiter.'

'ENOUGH!' shouted Obadiah.

Capstan had clearly hit a nerve.

'So anyway,' Obadiah continued, having regained control of his temper. 'I think the tour's over, but I do have just one more thing to show you,' and with a thin smile, he stepped between them, heading back towards the doorway they'd used to enter his secret subterranean lagoon. And as he did, he said, 'If you could follow me, everyone; but don't worry, it won't be long before you'll all be able to get your feet up.'

CHAPTER THIRTY FOUR

BACK INSIDE HIS subterranean apartment, Obadiah led them through a more normal-looking door which took them inside another cavern, but this one was already lit with what felt like natural light, and bore a remarkable resemblance to an ornate Japanese garden featuring a large rock pool in its centre surrounded by a dense variety of exotic-looking plants and shrubs.

As Capstan, Dewbush and Mallum stepped inside and began to take in their new surroundings, Obadiah said, 'This is where I keep my pet fish. Would any of you like to hazard a guess as to what species that might be?'

Obadiah gazed around at his guests, wondering if any of them looked as if they might know. But as none of them seemed to, he answered the question for himself.

'It's the Piranha!'

He again looked around at them, hoping to see signs of primeval fear become etched into their faces, but only Capstan seemed to show any signs of knowing what a Piranha was, and his sole outward sign of concern was that he momentarily raised one of his eyebrows.

243

'I must admit,' continued Obadiah, 'that I didn't know of the species myself until I discovered that a school of them had been sucked up by my vacuum trawler. And I was so impressed by how they were able to strip the flesh off almost any living creature in a matter of seconds that I decided to breed them here, as a sort of a hobby,' and he gestured down at the pool of crystal clear water which appeared to be crammed full of the metre-long prehistoric carnivores, along with their razor sharp teeth.

'On the subject of fish,' he continued, looking back up at his three guests as they continued to study the underwater monsters that seemed to circle each other just underneath the surface, 'does anyone know how many aquatic species there are in the known universe?'

Unsurprisingly, none of them did.

'Probably around a thousand,' he answered for himself again. 'And until recently they all lived on Earth. But although that's quite an interesting fact, it becomes far more so when compared to the number of species there were estimated to be living in Earth's oceans during their 20th Century.'

He stopped to see if anyone was going to offer a guess as to how many that may have been, but as none of them seemed to be all that interested, he continued.

'At that time it was thought that there were over two million! So, you may think it fair to accuse me of sucking up all of Earth's fish for my own financial gain, but from my perspective I'd say it's been more of an animal rescue mission. After all, humans do seem to have a nasty habit of devouring everything in their path, like one of their locust insects, with hardly a thought as to what that might mean for the wellbeing of the plants and animals they'd need for their own survival. So I see the work I've been doing as more…humanitarian, a word I've always thought to be rather contradictory, being that it generally involves cleaning up after what humans have already managed to screw up themselves. And although my work has so far seemed to be benefitting the human race, I can assure you that it isn't! For example, people may think that I bought the Meanz brand, moved baked bean production here and exported them back to Earth to ensure humans continued to have a great product at an even better price. However, what it actually means is that I'll be able to control Earth's supply of baked beans, and in very much the same way as I'll soon be able to control Earth's supply of fish.'

'What about the Final Fish Finger?' asked Dewbush, in a resentful tone. 'Why go to the trouble of stealing that when you already had all our fish?'

'Ah, yes, of course,' and he held it up for them all to gaze upon once more. 'The Final Fish Finger represents the last stage in my grand plan. My intention is to start manufacturing them again, and then to export them back to Earth in much the same way as I've been doing with my baked beans. You see, I know how popular they used to be, and their shape and size combined with the fact that they can easily be frozen makes them the ideal product for intergalactic export. And once the human species is again eating them by the tonne, and has become wholly reliant on them in the process, I'll simply pull the plug on both their production and the baked beans. And when I do, I'll be able to sit back and watch Earth starve to death, before the human species does the Universe a big favour and dissolves back into the primordial swamp from where it first came. However, I must admit that I've been having a little trouble duplicating the Fish Finger's crispy golden texture, which is why I had my Research and Development team run so many tests on it. But we made a breakthrough this morning, and we had planned on having the very first one made by end of play today; that was until you came along of course. But no matter, you've only set me back by a day or two, which is of little consequence, in the grand scheme of things.

'Now I really do feel the tour has come to an end,' he said, and placing the test tube containing the Final Fish Finger under his arm he clapped his hands twice, saying, 'but before I go, I think it's only fair that I keep my promise and give you the chance to get your feet up.'

As he said that, they heard the heavy flip-flop of

webbed feet coming from behind them.

Turning around, they saw three well-proportioned armed Gannar guards enter by the door they'd only just walked through themselves, stop, and stand to attention, presumably awaiting their next orders.

CHAPTER THIRTY FIVE

'SIR?'
          'Yes, Dewbush?'

'You know when Obadiah said that we'd be able to get our feet up after his tour?'

'What about it, Dewbush?'

'Well, to be honest sir, if I'd known he'd meant we'd be hung upside down above his flesh-eating pet fish with our hands tied behind our backs, I probably wouldn't have been so keen to have taken him up on the offer.'

'No, Dewbush. I doubt any of us would.'

Capstan, Dewbush and Mallum had indeed been hung upside down by their feet, and from a steel cable that stretched from wall to wall above the pool of piranhas. With the two Space Police officers still wearing their disguises, they looked like three wetsuits that had been hung out to dry on some sort of macabre washing line, with Dewbush in the middle and Capstan and Mallum dangling either side of him.

Obadiah had even been considerate enough to allow Capstan and Dewbush to keep their diver's masks on, so that they'd be able to watch the piranhas as they began eating the flesh off of their faces before they either passed out or drowned. However, prior to any of that happening, the tide had to come in. Ganymede's ocean was pulled by Jupiter's gravitational force, as the moon rotated around the giant planet, which was strong enough to have an effect on the water system flowing around Obadiah's subterranean retreat, about a mile beneath the ocean's surface.

So, until then, Obadiah had decided to leave them to hang there for a while, giving the opportunity for them to contemplate their fate. As he'd dispatched a number of Gannets using the very same method, he knew there was no way for them to escape, and had therefore decided to dismiss the guards who'd been so helpful in hanging them up.

And so it was that Capstan, Dewbush, and their brave Health and Safety Manager and part-time translator Mallum, whose eldest son they'd rescued just the day before from a freak dinghy boat accident, were staring down at a large number of metre-long piranha, which in turn were staring straight back up at them, looking increasingly desperate to start on their main dish of the day: two human beings with a Gannet on the side.

'Looks like the tide's coming in,' observed Dewbush, as the water's surface began to rise inextricably towards their heads.

'It would appear so,' commented Capstan, finding himself unable to stop worrying about his impending fate, and in particular how much having his head eaten by piranhas was going to hurt, and how long he'd have to put up with the pain before he either passed out or died. It was hardly the first time he'd found himself in such an awkward situation, but no matter how many times he had, he always found himself suffering from acute nervousness, probably in much the same way as an in-demand actor did who suffered from stage fright.

Still staring down at the fish, Dewbush said, 'It looks like this is it then, sir.'

'You could be right there, Dewbush,' replied Capstan, with philosophical acceptance of what seemed inevitable.

'I suppose at least we can talk to each other this time, sir. The last time we were in such a situation we had gags on. Do you remember, sir?'

'Indeed I do, Dewbush,' said Capstan, unsure how he could have forgotten, seeing that it had only been the week before, on Titan, inside what had turned out to be Lord Von Splotitty's recording studio which he also used for interrogation.

After having a last minute look around, Capstan asked, 'I don't suppose anyone has any idea as to how we might be able to escape?'

Initially his request was met only by silence, until Dewbush suggested, 'I suppose I could have a go at untying your hands with my teeth, like I did last time, sir?'

Despite not particularly wanting to have his

lieutenant slobber over his hands again, at least it was preferable to how he'd removed his gag the last time, which was basically to French kiss him until it came off. 'Do you think you could have a go, Dewbush?'

'I'll try, sir,' and with that, Dewbush heaved the top half of his body up so that his head was parallel with Capstan's waist, but their bodies kept spinning around making it virtually impossible for Dewbush to get anywhere near Capstan's hands. After a few moments of massive physical effort, he gave up and dropped back down.

'It's – no – use,' he gasped, trying to regain his breath, 'but I just can't hold myself up for long enough, sir.'

'Don't worry, Dewbush. At least you had a go.'

'May I make a suggestion?' asked Mallum, who until then had been dangling beside Dewbush without saying a word.

'By all means,' said Capstan.

'Well, I was thinking that perhaps we could have a go at untying each other's hands?'

'But we're too far away to be able to reach,' said Dewbush.

'Not if we could rock towards each other. Then, when we get close enough, one of us could grab hold of the other, whilst the other had a go at doing the untying.'

'You know what?' said Capstan. 'It just might

work!'

Despite being a little put out that he hadn't thought of it first, Dewbush agreed to have a go, and the three of them began wriggling themselves around in an effort to start rocking back and forth. But all that was happening was that their heads kept slamming in to each other's, which was doing nothing more than giving them all a bit of a headache.

'It's not working,' said Capstan, after Dewbush had head-butted him for the third time.

'Maybe if just one of us moves?' suggested Mallum. 'Then the one who's staying still can focus on keeping his body rotated so that his hands are facing the one who's trying to rock towards him.'

'OK, let's give it a go. Dewbush, if you try to keep your back facing me, I'll try to rock myself over towards you. But just be ready to grab me when I do!'

'Understood, sir!'

'Right then, here I go,' and as Capstan began to rock himself backwards and forwards so that his body would swing into Dewbush's, Dewbush did his best to keep his back facing Capstan, with the hands behind his back ready to grab his boss the moment he swung close enough.

Moments later, Dewbush called out, 'I think I've got you, sir!'

'You've actually got my balls, Dewbush,' said Capstan, clearly in some pain.

'Oh, sorry, sir. Shall I let go?'

With a quick glance down at the piranhas just under the surface of the water, which was now only about an inch away from the top of his head, with a slightly higher pitched voice than normal, Capstan said, 'I don't think we've got time to try again, Dewbush, but my hands are tied around my back, not my front, so you need to try and swivel me around so that I'm facing the other way.'

'I could always hold on to your penis instead, sir?'

'And how's that going to help?'

'I was just trying to think of what else I could hold on to, sir.'

'Try my diver's belt, Dewbush. You could then use that to turn me around.'

'Right. I think I've got that, sir!'

Grateful that Dewbush had finally let go of his balls, in a more normal sounding voice, Capstan said, 'OK, now work your way around the belt until I'm facing the other way.'

Another thirty seconds later, Dewbush managed to do that, giving cause for Capstan to say, 'Well done, Dewbush. Now, don't let go, whatever you do, and I'm going to have a go at untying you.'

'Right you are, sir.'

Another minute or two passed in silence as Capstan focused his mind on the task of untying his subordinate's hands, but without the luxury of being able to see what he was doing.

'It's working, sir,' said Dewbush, by way of encouragement as he could feel the binds around his wrists begin to loosen. 'It's definitely working!'

Another thirty seconds later and Dewbush announced, 'You've done it, sir! You've done it!' as he discarded the now untied rope into the water beneath.

'That's great, Dewbush. Now, if you can untie me, then I can untie Mallum, and then, hopefully, we'll be able to unhook our feet and use the wire to climb out without having our heads chewed off in the process.

CHAPTER THIRTY SIX

A BOUT FIVE MINUTES later, Capstan, Dewbush and Mallum had all managed to untie each other, and unhook their feet, and without falling into what was basically a rock pool of impending death had successfully used the wire cable to climb to safety and were now crouching down behind the door leading out into Obadiah's apartment, catching their breath as they did so.

'What are we going to do now, sir?' asked Dewbush, as soon as he felt able to.

It was a good question, but it wasn't one to which Capstan knew the answer. He'd been so focussed on not having his face feasted upon by flesh-eating piranha, he hadn't given a second thought to what they'd do were they to escape. 'I'm not sure, Dewbush, but somehow we need to find our way back up to the surface and then get the hell out of here.'

It was hardly the most helpful comment he'd ever made, being that it gave no mention as to how they'd be able to find their way out of Obadiah's subterranean apartment and get back up to the surface without being caught, so Dewbush thought he'd enquire about the alien lifeform who'd be most likely to stop them, and asked, 'Is Obadiah there? Can

255

anyone see him?'

Being closest to the door Mallum ever-so-quietly opened it, but only just enough to peer through the gap into the living area, and a moment later whispered, 'Yes, he's still there.'

'What's he doing?' asked Dewbush, as if it was important, somehow.

'Sitting behind his desk with his feet up, watching those damned TV monitors.'

Sensing an opportunity, Capstan asked, 'Do you think we'd be able to sneak past without him noticing?'

'Well, he didn't hear us when we first arrived, so it's possible,' answered Mallum, under his breath. 'But even if we are able to reach the lift without him hearing us, knowing that the entire place is monitored by hidden CCTV cameras, and that he spends half his life watching them, I'd have thought he'd definitely see us at some point.'

There was a momentary pause as the three of them considered the problem for a while, before Dewbush said, 'I think I've got an idea, sir.'

After Capstan had waited a good ten seconds for him to say what it was, he eventually realised that he was probably waiting for permission, and so said, 'Go on then.'

'Well, sir, you remember how he rewound the video footage from the cameras when he was looking for the time he'd first seen us?'

'Yes, and...?'

'I was thinking that if we waited for him to pop out and then simply rewound the film back and pressed play, he'd find himself watching recorded footage, not the live video he normally would.'

It really wasn't a bad idea, but Mallum could see a problem.

'But each camera shows the exact date and time. So he'd soon realise that he was watching recorded footage.'

'But would he though?' asked Dewbush. 'Especially if we wound it back to this time say two days ago, so only the date was different, not the time.'

'I think we should give it a go,' said Capstan, but only because he couldn't think of a better idea.

'What's he doing now?' asked Dewbush again.

'The same. He's just…no, hold on. He's moving!'

'Is he coming this way?' asked Capstan, glancing behind him, looking for somewhere to hide.

'No. He's gone off somewhere else.'

'OK,' said Capstan, 'I don't see that we have any choice. He'll be coming back to check on us soon, so let's get over to his desk, reverse the camera footage and then we can see if we can get the hell out of here without being spotted.'

'Before we go, sir, do you mind if I take my flippers off?' asked Dewbush. 'It's just that I think I'd be able to move around a lot more quietly without them.'

'Good idea, Dewbush,' said Capstan. 'I think I'll do the same. But we're going to need them later, so make sure you keep a hold of them for now.'

Once they'd both pulled their flippers off, Capstan signalled to Mallum that they were ready, and he eased the door open, just enough for them to slip through. After a very quick check to make sure the coast was definitely clear, he scurried over to the desk with Capstan and Dewbush following behind, and in a way that they'd never have been able to do had they still been wearing the flippers.

Reaching the desk, Capstan whispered, 'Does anyone know how to rewind the footage?'

'It shouldn't be too difficult, sir,' answered Dewbush, and stooping over the touch-tech desk he pressed the relevant rewind image in the bottom left hand of the screen, in the same way as Obadiah had done earlier. The three of them then began to watch as all the Gannars and Gannets started walking backwards at 20 times normal speed, and they kept doing so until the screens displayed the correct time, near enough, but on a different day.

When Dewbush took his finger off the touch-tech screen, Capstan said, 'That will do. Right, let's get out of here before he comes back!' and they all scurried their way over to the lift doors where they'd come in.

Once there, Mallum pressed the button to call it, while they waited, desperately hoping that the doors would open before Obadiah returned from wherever it was that he'd disappeared to.

As they crouched besides the lift doors, Dewbush noticed that the dining table had been laid since they'd first arrived, and there, lying beside a white plate with a knife and fork on either side along with a bowl of baked beans and some tomato ketchup was the Fish Finger they'd come all that way to find, still in its test tube, and looking very much as if it was about to be eaten, but this time by Obadiah himself.

'It's the Final Fish Finger, sir!'

'I can see, Dewbush.'

'Shall I get it, sir?'

'It's too risky. Obadiah could be back at any moment.'

'But we can't just leave it there to be eaten, sir!'

Unfortunately Dewbush was right, and as the lift door still hadn't opened, Capstan said, 'All right, but be quick!'

And quick he was. Without the burden of his flippers, Dewbush was able to race over to the table in a matter of seconds. But just as he arrived, he heard the sound of flip-flopping footsteps, and glancing up saw that it was Obadiah, heading back towards his desk.

Ducking his head down behind the tall dining chair at the front of the table, Dewbush glared over at Capstan and Mallum, and then lifted his index finger to his lips before pointing over towards where the sound of Gannar footsteps was coming from. But they'd already seen him, which should have been fairly obvious as they'd both taken on the expression of a couple of bunnies having their eyes tested for short-sightedness.

Just then, the lift doors opened with a quiet ping, but which to Capstan, Dewbush and Mallum sounded more like a giant-sized gong being used to let King Kong know that dinner was ready.

The three of them continued to stare at Obadiah with ever-widening eyes to see if he'd heard it, but all he did was sit down, lean back in his black leather executive's chair and continue to watch the wall of monitors, exactly as he'd been doing before.

Wasting not another moment, and certainly before the lift doors closed, Dewbush reached his hand up, grabbed the test tube with the Final Fish Finger inside, and after a very quick glance over to make sure Obadiah was still engrossed watching the bank of TV screens, he hurried back to the lift and slipped inside, just as Capstan and Mallum did the same. And as soon as the doors closed, Mallum pressed the button for the top floor.

'That was close!' said Capstan.

'Too close!' agreed Mallum.

'But we've got the Final Fish Finger!' exclaimed Dewbush, holding it up for them to see. 'And Obadiah couldn't have noticed that he was watching the footage from yesterday, else he'd have said something.'

'And let's hope that he doesn't!' said Capstan. 'At least not until we're a very long way from here!'

'Do you think we should put our flippers back on, sir?' asked Dewbush, staring down at his feet which looked rather odd, being that they had neither shoes nor socks on.

'Yes, of course,' said Capstan, who'd completely forgotten about them.

By the time the lift reached the top, they'd both managed to squeeze back into their flippers, and when the doors pinged open, Dewbush held the test tube discreetly by his side, with his thumb over the top so that the precious contents didn't fall out. And as nonchalantly as possible the three of them began making their way out, first through the door signposted "No Gannets", then past the line of factory workers' lifts, and then out into the security checkpoint area where what Mallum had said about it being a lot easier getting out than it was to get in proved to be true. There was no turnstile for them to navigate, and although there were still plenty of security guards in the immediate vicinity, with no alarms going off they seemed content enough to simply stand around making idle conversation with each other.

So it really wasn't long before the three of them

were making their way down the steep harbour wall gantry steps, with Capstan and Dewbush being as careful as possible not to trip over their flippers as they did so.

Staring down at the moored up boats below, Mallum was both relieved and delighted to see his dinghy, and more to the point that his two sons were still there, waiting for them. Even before they reached the pontoon they could see that the young sailors had already started to hoist the sails in preparation for a speedy departure; well, about as speedy a departure as one could make in a sixteen-foot sailing dinghy that didn't have an engine.

CHAPTER THIRTY SEVEN

SINCE COMING BACK from the toilet and resuming his favourite pastime, that of sitting with his feet up on his desk, watching the world go by, something he found even more enjoyable knowing that the world in question was his, and that he could watch it go by courtesy of two hundred and forty three CCTV cameras he'd had secretly installed when he'd had his underwater city built, Gorgnome Obadiah was having the strangest sense of déjà vu.

As he stared up at the wall of monitors, there was something about what he was doing that made him think he'd done it all before, but for the life of him he couldn't work out which part of what he was doing the feeling related to. It probably didn't help that his day was structured around a strict routine, during which he did exactly the same thing, at the same time, day in, day out. One of the side effects of living such a life was that he often felt a sense of having done things before; but he was just one of those people who liked routine, and the feeling of rooted security it gave him. It was only when he had to travel to another planet on business, or when he had domestic issues to deal with, like having two Space Police officers sneaking around his baked bean factory, attempting to steal the very

263

Fish Finger he'd only had stolen himself a couple of days before, that his routine had a tendency to fall apart, something he found to be most disconcerting, not to mention rather annoying.

So was that it? Was he feeling a sense of déjà vu because he was finally getting back into his normal routine after his trip to the Intergalactic Food Talks on Earth and having had to deal with the two Space Policemen shortly after he'd returned?

Somehow he didn't think it was. It was something else, but that had at least reminded him that it was probably about time to check on his flesh-eating pet piranhas to make sure they'd enjoyed their supper. Assuming they had, he'd also have to fish out any inedible leftovers from the water that could easily clog up the filtration system if left unattended, but at least he quite enjoyed doing that. The part he wasn't quite so keen on was having to look at whatever was left of the bodies. Taking the remaining body parts off the meat hooks he used was an irksome job he normally left to his gardener, but he'd only come the day before, and wasn't due in for another week.

He checked the time on one of the TV monitors. It had been an hour since he'd left them. The tide would have definitely come up by now, so at least they'd be dead. How much would be left would depend on how high the tide had risen.

With a heavy sigh, he lifted his feet off the desk

again and flip-flopped his way over to the door that led into his Japanese garden. When he got there, he paused. Whenever he reached this moment of checking in on his special guests, he never knew quite what to expect. There was a time a while back when he'd gone in too early, and the fish had only just started on the heads, and their lunch was still thrashing about in the most appalling fashion. Not a pleasant sight! Obadiah had never been one for watching people being eaten alive. He didn't have a problem with having people killed, of course: that was all part of being a planetary dictator, but he didn't like the sight of blood, especially when it was spurting out of gurgling Gannets' faces as they were being feasted on by a school of hungry piranha. So before going in, he listened at the door, and, not being able to hear anything, tentatively pushed it open to peer inside.

What he saw was a little surprising. Somehow his guests must have thrashed about so much that they'd managed to unhook their feet from the cable, as the stubs of their legs weren't there as they usually were. It had happened before, but only once, so it certainly was unusual. But at least that meant he didn't have half-eaten legs to stare at like he usually did. Feeling slightly relieved, he walked in and knelt down beside the fish pond to see how his pet piranha were doing, and if they'd enjoyed the taste of human flesh, for a change. Looking at them it was difficult to tell, but they'd certainly eaten them all up, as there was no sign of anything left over at all, which was also peculiar. His pet piranha had eaten everything, including the wetsuits, flippers and masks that had made up the humans' pathetic disguises. Clearly they must have been hungry; either that or they really liked the humans and ate them so fast they didn't stop to decide where the human ended and where the wetsuit, flippers and diver's mask began. With a fond, whimsical smile, Obadiah decided that he'd have to think of a way to get hold of some more humans for them to nibble at.

After he'd spent a few minutes enjoying the tranquillity of his subterranean Japanese garden, he began to feel hungry himself. It must be time for his own dinner, and today he was in for a bit of a treat. Instead of returning the Final Fish Finger to his moronically inept scientists to eat, the ones who'd been so easily fooled by the humans, he was going to eat it himself, and had asked his kitchen staff to leave it out for him, along with some cold baked beans and tomato ketchup. Baked beans and tomato ketchup were hardly his favourite food, but he wanted to eat the Final Fish Finger in the way it used to be eaten on Earth, all those years ago.

As he flip-flopped back to his elegant dining table, he noticed that it had been laid for one, as it always was, and that the baked beans and the tomato ketchup were there; but the Final Fish Finger wasn't.

It must be in the kitchen being heated up, he thought to himself. He hadn't asked them to, but maybe it was supposed to be eaten hot. He'd no idea. But as he thought that, a feeling of dread crawled down his spine, like a slug making its way over a cold kitchen floor in search of something to eat. Something definitely wasn't right! The feeling of déjà vu he'd had when watching the CCTV footage, the fact that his pet fish had eaten every last bit of their meal, including the Space Policemen's neoprene wetsuits, rubber flippers and diver's masks, and that the Final Fish Finger wasn't on the table as he'd specifically asked it to be…

They couldn't have escaped? he thought, but immediately ruled that out as an impossibility. If they had, and even if he hadn't heard them flip-flop their way past him, he'd at least seen them sneaking out on the TV monitors, *unless they'd re-wound the…*

He ran over to his desk, just as fast as his webbed feet would allow, and focused his gaze at the bottom corner of the monitor in the middle to check the displayed time. He then checked that against the time given on the touch tech desk. But they were the same, just about, and with a sense of relief he sat back down in his chair. He'd risked a lot telling the Space Policemen all about his master plan; how he'd stolen Earth's fish using his vacuum trawler and that his end goal was to be able to watch the human species descend into cannibalistic zombie chaos. He'd even admitted to having stolen their precious Final Fish Finger, and if they had escaped it would be a disaster! But he was clearly being unnecessarily paranoid. They hadn't escaped. His pet piranha must have simply enjoyed the taste of human so much that they'd eaten everything associated with them; either that or they like the taste of neoprene and latex rubber. As for the missing Final Fish Finger, it must simply have been taken by his kitchen staff to be warmed up.

But then, as he sat there, resuming his surveillance of the monitors, he had the feeling of déjà vu once again, and this time it was because he'd definitely seen the footage before, or something happening very much like it. A factory worker had just dropped a biscuit on the floor, but hadn't bothered to pick it up. The exact same thing had happened two days before, and at the exact same location inside the baked bean factory. He stared down at the time on the screen again. Not only had the Gannet dropped the biscuit on the floor in the same way and at the same place, he'd done it at the exact same time as well!

Obadiah stared at the time displayed on the screen again.

The time was right but…

His heart thudded hard in his chest, and as his pulse began pounding behind his ears he glared down at his touch-tech desk. The time was right, but the date! The date was two days ago! He'd been sitting there watching re-wound footage from the day when he'd arrived back from Earth. And that could only mean…

Before hitting the alarm for the second time that day, and further disrupting production, he had to be sure, and he fast-forwarded the footage to the present time, and then re-wound the system back by just half an hour. He clicked through the different camera images until he found the one filming inside his Japanese garden. He'd never monitored it before, as he'd never thought there was any need to. Clearly that had been a huge oversight on his behalf, as the footage featured the two Space Policemen and their traitorous friend unhooking their feet from the cable and then swinging their way to safety.

Cursing himself for having underestimated the two Space Policeman, especially that one from the 21st Century who had all the medals, he hit the alarm.

CHAPTER THIRTY EIGHT

IT WASN'T UNTIL Capstan, Dewbush, Mallum and his two children had spent a good half hour sailing back in the darkness to Hiriko Hainbat Gauza Flotatzaile - the City of Many Floating Things – that they heard the distant wail of a siren drift over the ocean towards them. By that time they were so far away from Obadiah and his flesh-eating fish, they'd only been able to hear it because the wind was blowing hard from behind them, the same stiff breeze that was enabling them to be carried home at such a swift pace.

The moment they arrived back, and Mallum brought the boat into the wind so that its sails flapped as it gently eased up against the pontoon, with a huge sense of relief Dewbush stepped out and turned to look back out to where they'd sailed from, and with joy in his heart, announced, 'It looks like we made it, sir! All safe and sound!'

Capstan, clambering his way out to join him, asked, 'Do you still have the Fish Finger, Dewbush?'

'I do, sir. It's right here!' and he held it out for Capstan to see.

'Then I'd say we *have* made it, Dewbush,' and the two of them took a moment to smile at each other.

When Mallum joined them on the pontoon, he too

gazed over to where they'd come from, but instead of sharing Capstan and Dewbush's joyful liberation, there was only cold dark fear running through his mind.

'It looks like *you* have made it,' he agreed 'but unfortunately, I doubt if the rest of us will fare so well. Obadiah will be none too pleased that we escaped, and he certainly won't be happy that you stole back his Fish Finger. I'd have thought that at this very moment in time he's assembling his private army, ready to head over here. And assuming you'll have gone by then, I can imagine he'll be taking out his retribution on myself and my family, and probably the rest of the Gannet population shortly afterwards.'

Capstan and Dewbush looked first at Mallum, and then down at his two children, Akinda and Kai, who were busying themselves stowing the dinghy's mainsail away, which they were doing a remarkably good job of, considering how dark it was.

'I'd not thought of that,' said Dewbush.

'Neither had I,' added Capstan, both sounding as if they'd just reversed over a much-loved tortoise by accident.

In the brief time they'd spent on Ganymede with Mallum and his young family, they'd grown close, especially to his two young boys.

'We can't leave them, sir,' said Dewbush, feeling the sharp heat of tears stabbing at his eyes.

'You're right, Lieutenant. We can't, and we won't!'

271

Having made that decision, Capstan turned to stare up at their Space Police car, still parked on Mallum's roof.

'How many guns do we have with us, Dewbush?'

'We've got our normal two 12mm Decapitators which we left in the car, and then there are two 16mm Exterminators under the back seat. We've also got six hand-grenades and a few gas canisters as well, sir.'

'And ammunition?'

'A fair amount, sir, but probably not enough to fend off an entire private army.'

'No, but at least we'll be able to make a stand.'

'Yes, sir. But I suspect it will be a final stand though.'

'Much like the Fish Finger,' said Capstan, and turned to give Dewbush a smile of good old-fashioned British steadfast determination in the face of what appeared to be overwhelming odds.

Although Mallum was delighted to hear that they were going to stay, and that they were prepared to stand with them, side by side, until the bitter end, he did however have one rather obvious question.

'But isn't there some way you could call for backup?'

Dewbush looked over at him.

'Unfortunately, our phones don't work this far away from Earth.'

But Capstan thought there must be some way to get

a message out to the UKA Space Police Station orbiting Earth, other than via mobile phone. After all, this was the 25th Century! And with that in mind, he asked, 'Couldn't we send them an email, or something?'

'Well, yes, sir, we could, but it would take a while to get there.'

'But I thought email was instant?'

'Er, no, sir. You're thinking of Intergalactic Instant Messaging, sir.'

'Well, couldn't we "Intergalactic Instant Message" them then?'

'I suppose we could try using Slaptwat, sir.'

'Slaptwat?'

'Yes, sir. It's the latest social media app that lets you send messages to anyone in the universe, but I doubt if Space Police has signed up for it yet. It's only been out for a couple of months.'

'Isn't there an older version of something they might use?'

'Actually, sir, there are two others that are a little similar.'

'And what are they?'

'Catflap and Buttcrack, sir.'

'And what's the difference between Catflap, Buttcrack, and the other one?'

'Well, sir, they all allow you to send messages to people anywhere in the universe, including photos and videos, but Slaptwat deletes every message just two seconds after it's been received.'

'I see,' said Capstan, a little confused. 'But what's the point of sending someone a photo or a video for it to be deleted two seconds later?'

'Social media has become about living in the moment, sir. Catflap and Buttcrack were OK, but they never had any social immediacy about them.'

'Social immediacy?' asked Capstan.

'That's right, sir. But anyway, I doubt if Space Police has signed up to those either, so I can't see how they'd be of much use.'

Capstan wasn't going to give up that easily.

'Couldn't you send a message out to one of your friends using Slapcrap, or whatever it was called, and ask them to call Space Police on your behalf and tell them that we need backup?'

'That's not a bad idea, sir!' answered Dewbush, and pulled out his touch-tech PalmPad from his wetsuit sleeve, where he must have been keeping it all that time. 'Give me just one moment, sir,' and with that he woke the device up, darted his thumbs around the screen for all of three seconds before putting it away, and looked up at Capstan to say, 'All done, sir!'

'Really?' asked Capstan, unsure how he could have sent anything out so quickly.

'Yes, sir.'

'So, you've just sent a message to one of your

friends on Earth asking them to contact Space Police and to tell them that we needed backup, here on Ganymede?'

'I did, sir, although I did also mention that we'd found the Final Fish Finger, and that it was Gorgnome Obadiah who'd stolen it.'

'OK, good,' said Capstan.

'And I told them how he'd used a vacuum trawler to suck up half the oceans' supply of fish, and that's what he's now planning to sell back to Earth, but at five times the price.'

'Great.'

'I also added the part about Obadiah taking us prisoner, and that he'd attempted to have us eaten alive by flesh-eating piranha, but that we managed to escape, stealing back the Final Fish Finger as we did, and that we're now holed up on Hiriko Hainbat Gauza Flotatzaile, otherwise known as the City of Many Floating Things, where we're about to be attacked by his private army.'

'Anything else?'

'Only that I sent it out to all my friends, sir; not just one of them. I thought that way there'd be more chance that someone would be able to read it before it was automatically deleted.'

'Fantastic,' replied Capstan, and after waiting another moment to see if he'd managed to include any other useful information to the message, like what they'd been wearing when they'd been taken prisoner, or exactly where Dewbush had grabbed him when they were trying to escape, eventually asked, 'And you think that will work, do you Dewbush?'

'Oh, I'm sure it will, sir!'

'Right then,' said Capstan, and in the certain knowledge that they were all going to die, and with as much optimism as he thought was possible, given the circumstances, said, 'Then I suggest we get all the guns and ammo out from the car, and maybe we could build some sort of a barricade here…somewhere. No doubt we'll then easily be able to fend off Obadiah's private army whilst giving our Space Police re-enforcements plenty of time to get the message and make the trip over.'

CHAPTER THIRTY NINE

PRESIDENT OF EARTH, Dick Müller IV, had had a busy day. He hadn't actually done anything, nothing productive at least, but he'd been extremely busy doing it nonetheless. That was why he'd only just had the chance to sit down for his evening meal at the end of his rather long antique mahogany dining table, the one inside his lavish private apartment within the residential area of the White House, all ready to enjoy the meal his wife-bot Series 4000 called Susan had just placed in front of him, the very same one she'd spent the last three and a half hours cooking for him in the kitchen.

'This looks delicious,' he said, gazing down at it as his mouth began to salivate in anticipation of getting stuck in.

'Thank you, darling,' replied Susan, adding, 'It's Beef Bourguignon,' as she took her seat at the opposite end of the table. In front of her was nothing more than a single glass of water. The President's wife-bot made a remarkably convincing human female and had been designed to perform every possible action necessary to fulfil the marital obligations of a real wife, but there were three things her designers hadn't felt it necessary for her to do; eat food, digest it, and then

277

poo it out the other end. However, wife-bots were able to drink from a glass, at least the latest 4000 series were. This advanced humanoid feature was part of a social upgrade package which also included a programming function that allowed them to chat about incredibly boring subject matter like the weather, the correct way to peel a potato, and the latest celebrity gossip, as if it was all absolutely fascinating.

'Well, it smells great,' said Müller, still gazing down at it. 'Could you pass the salt?'

Susan stared at him, and after taking a sip from her water said, 'I think you'll find that it's been perfectly seasoned already, darling.'

'I'm sure that it has, darling, but you know how I like a lot of salt with my food.'

'Of course, darling, which was why I added 0.025 grams more than the recipe required.'

'Thank you, darling, but as you know, I always like to add more just before I eat it.'

'Then I suggest you taste it first, darling, to see if it does need more.'

'Can you please just pass the salt?'

Müller was beginning to lose his temper. He'd never liked being told what to do, or in this instance what not to do, especially over something as trivial as adding salt to his meal, which was probably the reason behind the failure of at least half of his marriages. But this relationship was different. For a start, they weren't married, and secondly, she wasn't human.

Susan fixed a vacant stare at him. No part of her body moved, not even her eyelids, despite the fact that they were programmed to blink every five seconds.

But it took only ten seconds for Müller to back down. He'd seen first-hand what she was capable of when faced with a situation of human antagonistic confrontation, and although there were no golf clubs around, at least not within grabbing distance, there were two tall silver candlesticks right in the middle of the table, and numerous other objet d'art dotted around the room, all of which could make admirable weapons of choice. So instead of continuing with the discussion about whether or not he should be allowed to add salt to his meal, he simply started eating it whilst making the appropriate noises of appreciation, before saying, 'You were right, darling. It is seasoned to perfection!' but without daring to look back up at her.

Just then there was a knock at the door on the far side of the room, behind where Müller was sitting.

'You must be joking!' he muttered, although he was secretly pleased as he could still feel his wife-bot's eyes boring into him. If she was going to launch herself over the table, picking up the two candlesticks along the way to begin using him as a kettle drum to play out the baseline to the national anthem, it would be useful to have someone on hand to help take her batteries out.

But as it turned out, just the sound of knocking at the door was enough to switch her programming function from "extreme passive aggression" to that of "answering the door", and she stopped staring at Müller and with her most charming home-baked smile said, 'I'll get that, darling,' and she pushed her chair away from the table, stood up and headed over to see who was there.

'Thanks, darling,' said Müller with relief, and was about to continue enjoying his meal when he realised who it probably was, and called out, 'but if it's that idiot Chief of Staff of mine, tell him I'm not in, and even if I am, it's well past five o'clock and anything he has to bore me with can wait till the morning.'

Opening the door, Susan said, 'Hello, Gavin! How are you this evening?'

'Oh, hello, Susan. Very well, thank you. Sorry to come round so late. Is he in?'

'He's having his dinner, but he's not in a very good mood, I'm afraid.'

'Ah, well, maybe I'd better come back in the morning then.'

'Don't be silly. Just go on in. You can chat to him while he's eating,' and she stepped to one side, calling out, 'It's Gavin to see you, darling.'

Glancing around to see that it was his Chief of Staff after all, Müller said, 'Gavin! How absolutely wonderful!' but without standing up. 'I haven't seen you for what – it must be hours now. How've you been?'

'Oh, fine thank you, Mr President, and sorry for coming around so late.'

'That's not a problem, Gavin, really it isn't. However, if you decide to do it again I'll cut your balls off and give them to Susan. No doubt she'll be able to rustle something up with them in the kitchen.

Gavin glanced over at Susan, who was walking beside him, all the time staring at him as he went, almost as if she'd already started accessing her recipe database to see which one could benefit most from having human testicles included as a key ingredient.

When they reached the table she stopped, turned to him and asked, 'Can I get you anything to eat, Gavin? Dumplings, perhaps?'

Taking a half-step away from her, Gavin said, 'Er, thank you, Susan, but no. I've, er, only just eaten,' before thinking to say thank you again.

With Susan still staring straight at him, he decided to push on with what he'd come to talk to his President about. He found his Commander-in-Chief intimidating enough, but at least he could read his emotions and react accordingly. His new wife-bot was something else entirely. She always appeared warm and welcoming on the outside, but he was very much aware that underneath her amicable façade was basically a binary computer whose operating system was based on nothing more than a choice between a 0 or a 1, which didn't leave a lot of wriggle room in between.

'Mr President, a report's just come in from Space Police that the Final Fish Finger has been found, sir!'

'The Final Fish Finger has been found?' repeated Müller, but only because he couldn't quite believe he was having his evening meal interrupted simply to be told such a trivial and decidedly dull item of news.

'It has, Mr President!'

'Really?'

'Yes, Mr President!'

'Wow! That's just great. I'm so pleased you came all the way up here to tell me. Now, are you going to leave through the door you came in by, or do I need to call security and have you thrown out of the nearest window?'

'B-but Mr President, sir, it was the location at which it was found that is of interest.'

'Let me guess. At the bottom of a freezer in the frozen food section of a local supermarket?'

'No, Mr President. It was found on Ganymede!'

'Ganymede?'

'Yes, Mr President. And the Space Police report states that the suspect behind its theft is none other than Gorgnome Obadiah!'

'Really?' said Müller, but with considerable more

sincerity that time.

As Gavin pulled out his touch-tech PalmPad to check the details, he added, 'And he's also under suspicion of stealing half of Earth's fish using what's being termed a "vacuum trawler". And it's those fish he's now proposing to sell back to us at five times the going rate.'

'Anything else?' asked Müller, beginning to think that Christmas really had come early that year.

'Yes, Mr President. There are two Space Police officers on the planet at this precise moment in time calling for back-up. Apparently, they were taken prisoner by Obadiah who attempted to have them eaten alive by flesh-eating piranha. However, they managed to escape and took the Final Fish Finger with them. They're now holed up on Hiriko Hainbat Gauza Flotatzaile, otherwise known as the City of Many Floating Things, where they're readying themselves to be attacked by Obadiah's private army.'

Müller thought for a moment before saying, 'Get me Vice President Pollock on the phone.'

'Oh, er…he's still officially missing in action, Mr President, after last week's attack of the Mammary Clans.'

'Oh yes. So he is. Then get me the Secretary of Defence.'

'Which one, Mr President?'

'What do you mean, which one?'

'Well, the last one is in intensive care after being involved in a freak yachting accident, and although his replacement has been both nominated and approved, he doesn't seem too keen to accept.'

'Then who's in charge of our armed forces then?'

'Er, you are, Mr President, being that you're our Commander-in-Chief.'

'Oh yes, I'd forgotten about that. Right! Get me on the line to whoever I need to speak to. I want our entire intergalactic space fleet sent over to Ganymede, and I want them sent over NOW!'

CHAPTER FORTY

'I'M NOT SURE if we're going to be able to hold them off for much longer, sir,' said Dewbush, ducking back down behind their Space Police car. He'd just successfully blown the head off one of twelve power boat drivers, all members of Obadiah's private army, and all attempting to moor up alongside Mallum's dinghy to re-capture their three escaped prisoners and to take back possession of the Final Fish Finger, as ordered.

As another round of bullets ricocheted off the car, perhaps fired by one of the boats' crew who was feeling a little miffed to see his friend's head being replaced by nothing more than a pulsating fountain of gurgling blood, Capstan said, 'I'm not sure either, Dewbush.'

Since the fighting had started, Capstan had become increasingly impressed by his lieutenant's marksmanship. Dewbush had so far killed at least ten members of Obadiah's private army and was certainly making up for Capstan's own lack of ability. In fact, if it wasn't for his MDK 12mm Decapitator being armed with self-guiding bullets, he doubted if he'd have hit anything at all. But as it was, they'd been doing a decent enough job of preventing any of the

285

powerboats from landing, and as their adversaries only seemed to be armed with machine guns loaded with normal bullets, and the Space Police car was made of a special composite material that was both light and bulletproof, so far they'd been safe enough sheltering themselves behind it.

'How long do you think it will be before your backup arrives?' asked Mallum, whose wife and children were hiding behind the sofa in their cabin. He'd been given one of their spare MDK 16mm Exterminators and had joined the two Space Policemen behind their car which Dewbush had re-parked on the pontoon, halfway between Mallum's dinghy and his cabin. After all, it made for the perfect barricade, and saved them a fair amount of time having to build another one.

'It shouldn't be long now,' said Capstan, unable to tell him what he really thought, which was that Dewbush sending a message via some intergalactic mobile social media app to all his friends as a way to call for Space Police backup was hardly likely to have worked, especially as that message was going to delete itself just two seconds after it had been received.

'Do you think I should try sending another Slaptwat message, sir?'

'I think it's probably a little late for that, Dewbush.'

As a bullet whizzed directly over Dewbush's head, he said, 'You're probably right, sir.'

And Capstan was right. They'd been very fortunate in that it had taken a good two hours for Obadiah's private army to arrive. That was because most of them had thought the alarm was for either an earthquake or a fire, and had subsequently spent at least half an hour lining up at Mandau's various fire assembly points to be counted. Once they'd been told that the alarm was for escaped prisoners who needed to be re-captured at all costs, it had taken them even longer to decide who was going to go in which boat, and more importantly, which one of them was going to drive.

This had given Capstan and Dewbush plenty of time to prepare themselves for the expected onslaught. They'd used that time to change back into their suits and gravity-coats, arm themselves with the various guns, ammo, hand-grenades and gas canisters from under the back seat of the car, and to give Mallum a quick lesson in how to load, re-load and fire the MDK Exterminator.

But despite all that, they were significantly out-numbered, and it would only be a matter of minutes before they were overrun.

'Shall I try throwing another hand-grenade, sir?' asked Dewbush, as the machine gun fire drew ever closer.

'How many do we have left?' asked Capstan.

'Just the one, sir.'

'OK, well, maybe we should save that for when we

run out of ammo.'

'What about using one of the gas canisters? We've still got three of them.'

'Why not, Dewbush! But keep one for the very end. We might need it to help us retreat.'

Dewbush glanced at the wooden cabin behind them. It was hardly a concrete bunker, and which gave him reason to ask, 'Retreat to where, sir?'

It was a good question, and one to which Capstan didn't have an answer, so he said, 'Just keep one till the end, Dewbush, in case we need it for something.'

'Right you are, sir,' and with that, Dewbush plucked one of the remaining gas canisters from its padded suitcase, pulled out the pin and lobbed it high over towards the nearest speed boat into which it landed with perfect precision, engulfing it in a blanket of thick white smoke.

'Good shot, Dewbush!' commented Capstan, who'd taken a chance to see where it landed by peering through the front windows of their Space Police car.

'Thank you, sir! I used to play intergalactic cricket at school, and my PE teacher always said I was good at throwing.'

'I assume intergalactic cricket is like normal cricket, but just played...intergalactically?' asked Capstan, out of curiosity.

'I suppose so, sir,' answered Dewbush, although he'd never heard of any other version, apart from intergalactic rounders, and intergalactic baseball of course, both of which he had to admit were very similar.

As another heavy burst of gun fire rattled into, and then straight off of the car, a huge explosion rocked the entire pontoon, leaving them to be showered with wooden debris a moment or two later.

Recognising one of the pieces that had first landed on his head before falling into his lap, Mallum picked it up and exclaimed, 'They've just blown up my dinghy!'

'Well, you know what that means, don't you?' said Capstan.

'I certainly do,' continued Mallum. 'It means that I've now got no way of getting into work!'

'It means,' continued Capstan, 'that they've now got explosives as well as guns!'

'And the car isn't bomb proof, sir,' added Dewbush, understanding the full significance of the explosion.

'I suggest a final push is in order,' said Capstan. 'That way we may be able to drive them back far enough for them not to be able to lob hand-grenades at us.'

'If they are hand-grenades, sir.'

'Well, Dewbush, they go bang, and they blow stuff up, so whatever they are, we really don't want them anywhere near us.'

'No, sir.'

'I suggest we count to three and then start shooting back at them, all at the same time. Agreed?'

Dewbush and Mallum nodded.

'OK. One, and two, and…'

'Hold on, sir,' said Dewbush, 'my phone's ringing,' and before waiting for permission to answer it he lifted his watch to his mouth. But with so much noise going on around them, he had to raise his voice, and Capstan could only hear one side of the conversation.

'Hello? Yes, I'm Lieutenant Dewbush of UKA Space Police. That was me, yes. Really? That's great news! Thank you! We look forward to seeing you soon then. OK, great! Bye for now.'

With that, he ended the call and grinned over at Capstan.

'That was our back-up sir. They just called to say that they received my message and that they'll be here any minute.'

With a huge sigh of relief, Capstan exclaimed, 'Thank God for that!'

'Oh, and they've got with them Earth's entire fleet of intergalactic warships, so I reckon we'll be OK now, sir.'

'What was that social media app called again?' asked Capstan.

'What, Slaptwat, sir?'

'That's the one. Remind me to download it when all

this is over, will you? It sounds like something I should have, just in case I ever find myself in a similar situation.'

'Of course, sir. And then I'll be able to send you a friendship request.'

Capstan glanced over at Dewbush. He wasn't sure if he'd describe him as a friend. A work colleague, obviously, but a friend? Somehow the idea of Dewbush being described as one didn't feel right. However, as he was the only person he had any sort of a relationship with in the 25th Century, there was a strong possibility that he was, or at least should be considered as one, until he'd had a chance to do a little more socialising outside of the tightknit community that was the United Kingdom of America's Space Police Force in order to find someone a little more suitable.

CHAPTER FORTY ONE

SHORTLY AFTER Dewbush had ended the call, the sound of automatic gunfire and outboard motors was joined by the approaching whine of Space Police sirens, causing those firing the guns to stop doing so and stare up towards where the sound was coming from. What they saw was enough for them to come to a decision that a general cease fire was in order, as although they were happy enough to shoot at a couple of Space Policeman, the hundred or so descending down towards them meant that they were soon to be vastly outnumbered. Their decision was further justified when they saw that behind the mass of Space Police cars came what appeared to be Earth's entire Intergalactic Starfleet, and as Obadiah hadn't mentioned anything about them having to defend Ganymede against an alien invasion, they were more than happy to drop their weapons and raise their hands above their heads by way of surrendering, even before anyone had asked them to.

'I thought that all went rather well,' said Dewbush, once it was clear that the battle was over and it was safe for them to emerge from behind the car.

But Capstan thought it could have gone a lot better. Surviving being captured by a psychotic planetary dictator, hung upside down above a pool of flesh-eating fish, and nearly having his head blown off by a bunch of machinegun- wielding aquatic aliens may have been his lieutenant's idea of things going "rather well", but they weren't his. His idea of things going "rather well" was when he beat someone at Scrabble. But at least they'd come out of it in one piece, and along the way they'd managed to unmask the mastermind behind the theft of the Final Fish Finger, and uncover the plot to control and then cut off Earth's fish finger and baked bean supply in the hope that the human species would be reduced to a huddled mass who'd have no choice but to turn to cannibalism in order to survive. He doubted it would have ever come to that, as humans had a tendency to be able to think their way out of sticky situations, and there were a number of other things for them to eat apart from fish fingers and baked beans, like pizza, for example. But even so, it had been a diabolical plot, and one that they'd successfully managed to thwart.

Mallum, who also now stood up from behind the car, wasn't convinced it had turned out "rather well" either. Yes, he was alive, and when he saw his wife and children emerge unharmed from their floating cabin to join them on the pontoon he was overcome with joyful emotion, but his beloved dinghy had been virtually destroyed during the hostilities.

After he embraced his family, Capstan and

Dewbush watched as they all stared down at what was left of the dinghy, which wasn't much.

'Shame about his boat, sir,' commented Dewbush.

'Yes, but I'm sure he'll be able to put it back together, eventually,' said Capstan.

'But not in time to get in to work tomorrow though, sir, which will mean that Obadiah will probably fire him.'

Capstan gazed off in the direction of Mundau, where the baked bean factory was, along with Obadiah's subterranean apartment, his giant-sized vacuum trawler and his flesh-eating pet fish.

'Somehow I suspect our Mr Obadiah is going to have other things to worry about other than the production of baked beans and the hiring and firing of staff; at least, he will once we get back over there, arrest him and submit our report, along with the corroborating evidence.'

'You mean, the Final Fish Finger, sir?' asked Dewbush, holding it up for them to look at.

'Yes, that's exactly the corroborating evidence I was thinking of, Dewbush. But I see no reason why the baked bean factory won't be able to keep running after Obadiah's behind bars where he belongs. And if that's the case, then I'm sure they'll be needing someone who knows his way around the place to help manage it.'

With that, Capstan turned to look over at Mallum

and his family who'd already begun fishing bits of their dinghy out of the water. 'And I suggest we mention Mallum in our report,' continued Capstan. 'After all, we couldn't have done it without him.'

'I completely agree, sir!'

'And I see no reason why we can't also put his name forward as being the perfect candidate for taking over the management of the baked bean factory. But for now we need to get back over to Mandau, arrest Obadiah, and get both him and the Fish Finger back to Earth as quickly as possible.'

They took a moment to stare at the Fish Finger, still inside its test tube. It didn't look quite as crisp and golden as it had when they'd first seen it, lying on the plate in the baked bean factory's lab; in fact it was looking a little worse for ware, saggy even, and a bit loose at the seams, like Bagpuss waking up after an all-night pyjama party.

'Maybe we should try to find some ice to put it in, before we head back, sir?'

'I can't imagine anyone's got any ice around here, Dewbush.'

'Mallum might have some, sir.'

They both looked over to see that he was now on his knees, lamenting over the loss of his beloved dinghy as he tried joining various pieces of its wreckage together, but without much luck.

'Now might not be a good time, Dewbush.'

'What about Obadiah, sir?'

'What about him?'

'He's probably got some ice in his apartment, sir.'

'That's a very strong possibility, Dewbush. C'mon, let's head back over there. We can ask him after we've formally charged him, and then we can make for home.'

'But what about Mallum's dinghy, sir?'

'To be honest, Dewbush, I think it's probably a little beyond repair, but I suppose we could always buy him some glue before we leave.'

Dewbush liked that idea, and as they climbed into their Space Police car to fly over to Mandau to formally charge Gorgnome Obadiah with the theft of the Final Fish Finger as well as half of Earth's supply of fish, Dewbush suggested to Capstan that when they bought the glue, maybe they could buy some Sellotape for him as well.

Detective Inspector Capstan returns in
Space Police: The Toaster That Time Forgot

ABOUT THE AUTHOR

BORN IN a US Navy hospital in California, David spent the first eight years of his life being transported from one country to another, before ending up in a three bedroom semi-detached house in Devon, on the South Coast of England.

David's father, a devout Navy Commander, and his Mother, a loyal Christian missionary, then decided to pack him off to an all-boys boarding school in Surrey, where they thought it would be fun for him to take up ballet. Once there, he showed a remarkable aptitude for dance and, being the only boy in the school to learn, found numerous opportunities to demonstrate the many and varied movements he'd been taught, normally whilst fending off attacks from his classroom chums who seemed unable to appreciate the skill required to turn around in circles, without falling over.

Meanwhile, his father began to push him down the more regimented path towards becoming a trained assassin, and spent the school holidays teaching him how to use an air rifle. Over the years, and with his father's expert tuition, he became a proficient marksman, managing to shoot a number of things directly in the head. His most common targets were birds but also extended to those less obvious, including his brother, sister, an uncle who popped in for tea, and several un-suspecting neighbours caught doing some gardening.

Horrified by the prospect of her youngest son spending his adult life travelling the world to indiscriminately kill people, for no particular reason, his mother intensified her efforts for him to enter the more highbrow world of the theatre by applying him to enter for the Royal Ballet. But after his twenty minute audition, during which time he jumped and twirled just as high and as fast as he possibly could, the three ballet aficionados who'd stared at him throughout with unhidden incredulity, proclaimed to his proud mother that the best and only role they could offer him would be that of, "Third Tree from the Left" during their next performance of Pinocchio, but that would involve him being cut down, with an axe, during the opening scene. Furthermore, they'd be unable to guarantee his safety as the director had decided to use a real axe instead of the normal foam rubber one, to add to the drama of an otherwise rather staid production.

A few weeks later, and unable to find any suitable life insurance, David's mother gave up her dream for him to become a famed Primo Ballerino and left him to his own devices.

And so it was, that with a sense of freedom little before known, he enrolled himself at a local college to study Chain Smoking, Under-Age Drinking, Drug

Abuse and Fornication but forgot all about his core academic subjects. Subsequently he failed his 'A' Levels and moved to live in a tent in Dorking where he picked up with his more practised skills whilst working as a Barbed Wire Fencer.

Having being able to survive the hurricane of '87, the one that took down every tree within a fifty mile radius of his tent, he felt blessed, and must have been destined for greater things, other than sleeping rough during the night and being repeatedly stabbed by hard to control pieces of metal during the day. So he talked his way onto a Business Degree Course at the University of Southampton.

After three years of intensive study and to the surprise of just about everyone, he graduated with a 2:1 and spent the next ten years working in several incomprehensibly depressing sales jobs in Central London, before setting up his own recruitment firm.

Seven highly profitable years later, during which time he married and had two children, the Credit Crunch hit, which ended that particular episode of his career.

It's at this point he decided to become a writer which is where you find him now, happily married and living in London with his young family.

When not writing he spends his time attempting to persuade his wife that she really doesn't need to buy the entire contents of Ikea, even if there is a sale on.

And when there are no items of flat-packed furniture for him to assemble he enjoys writing, base-jumping, and drawing up plans to demolish his house to build the world's largest charity shop.

www.david-blake.com

Printed in Great Britain
by Amazon